"I REMEMBER THOSE NIGHTS WHEN I WAS YOUNG IN LA—THE SMELL OF SWEAT AND PISS IN GRIMY CLUBS AND A CREATURE FLOATING TOWARD YOU THAT SUMMED UP THE GLAMOUR AND GLORY OF IT ALL......LIKE A YOUNG DIANA ROSS, SEAN DELEAR WAS ALL FEROCITY AND VULNERA-BILITY......SINGING 'ALL TOMORROW'S PARTIES' IN A THROATY CROON AND FLUTTERING DRUG STORE MAKEUP AISLE EYELASHES.........THESE DIARIES FINALLY GIVE ME THE BACKSTORY."

— Rick Owens

"Sean D told me about the diary but you can't fathom the excitement, growth, pain, and discovery etched onto those pages until you read them for yourself. The lack of shame describing her youthful sex adventures, the natural courage Sean D always had, it's all in the diary."

— Kembra Pfahler

"His magic was erasing context, no matter what scene he was in. Sean DeLear's teenage diary reveals how he was born with this unique power, combined with an incredible confidence that made his entire life a performance."

— Shayne Oliver

"Sean D wasn't challenging gender; he was expanding the spectrum of what it meant to be a man."

— Scott Ewalt

"Yes, this is a teenage diary, with all the attendant self-discovery, angst, and first-time social experiments. What makes it such fascinating reading is the realization that, not that long ago, all of it would have had to stay on the q.t. But no more, I'm happy to say. This is "coming out" for real, not the moment of family confession so many other narratives mistake it for. It documents a self-constructed cosmology without the help of any counselor and only desire as its guide. Let's treasure it."

— Bruce Benderson

"This diary is a window to the beautifully banal perspective of a sassy, fourteen-year-old adult from the Valley discovering male sex, obsession, and romantic love. A boy that follows his instincts in innocent grace, playfulness, and honesty. These pages present a fearless trajectory full of lust for life."
— Markus Zizenbacher

"What a peek into the queer teenage ping pong mind. School, paper route, and cock to name a few obsessions. The essence of the adult Sean DeLear I knew still contained the sweetness and cunning spark of the child of his private diaries. Couldn't put it down."
— Kid Congo Powers

"Horny for life and just plain horny, Sean DeLear's diary has the glorious brightness of teendom. Its off-rhythms of transcription, daydream, and self-mythologizing provide a record of its time, but anyone who remembers the tuned-up hopes of being young, brave, and reckless will recognize the feelings. It's all here: the restless formation of self, the sexual misadventures, the sweet swagger, the drift of ambition, and the mightiness of just being. It's fun as hell."
— Nate Lippens

"1979. What a magical year. Some of the most iconic disco records were released that year, and in many ways it was the calm before the storm. Reading Sean DeLear's diary is really a reflection of a time of freedom, rebellion, sexual liberation, dance, and decadence, through the eyes of an unapologetic Black queer artist who never let the restraints of others limit his lust for life. A truly transgressive spirit."
— Honey Dijon

"I knew Sean D from going out in LA. Sooooo fab. He was always a force, both beauty and energy. This daily account of his empowered queer youth is a rare gift."
— Telfar Clemens

This book is presented by Sean DeLear International, a partnership between Cesar Padilla, Michael Bullock, and Markus Zizenbacher, dedicated to sharing the life and art of their friend.

Published by Semiotext(e)
PO BOX 629, South Pasadena, CA 91031
www.semiotexte.com

Special thanks to Mike Hoffman, Aaron Smart, Markus Zizenbacher, Philipp Teuchtler, Kid Congo Powers and the Pink Monkeybirds, Thomas and Niki Wildner, Paul Graves, Jeppe Laursen, Paul Kopkau, Felix Burrichter, Richard Pursel, Philip Littell, Ron Athey, Roddy Bottum, Gert Jonkers, Jop van Bennekom, Brontez Purnell, Eric Robertson, Radford Brown, Lia Gangitano, Rick Owens, Scott Ewalt, Kembra Pfahler, Sophie Mörner, Jaime Wolf, Tyler Mariano, and BUTT magazine

Photographs of Sean DeLear courtesy of Markus Zizenbacher
Cover Design: Lauren Mackler
Design: Hedi El Kholti

ISBN: 978-1-63590-183-2

Distributed by the MIT Press, Cambridge, MA. and London, England
Printed in the United States of America

10 9 8 7 6 5 4 3 2

I Could Not Believe It: The 1979 Teenage Diaries of Sean DeLear

Edited by Michael Bullock
and Cesar Padilla

Introduction
by Brontez Purnell

MOTHER, forever, for sure and for always

I met Sean DeLear when I was twenty-four, in this house across from the Eagle in Los Angeles—I remember Sean talking about the LA scene, me asking him if he had a Germs burn (I don't remember the answer), but also being very struck by the fact that up until that point I had probably only met a couple dozen Black punks but never anyone of Sean De's age and with their poise. Even in Stripped Bare House at 2 a.m. and being festive she just commanded this kind of magic and glamour—it was definitely something to reach for and to aspire to. We don't always clock these things when we are younger, but the mere presence of her let me be hip to the fact that I could be beautiful, Black, and punk forever—and in fact, it would be the best possible path to take.

It had been mentioned to me by Alice Bag (of the Bags, duh) that Sean was amongst the "First 50"—that seminal group of LA kids who comprised of the first freaks to go to punk shows in Los Angeles and the genius LA punk. I being a total-poser '90s punk can't even wrap my head around the dopamine effect of being in the mix when it all felt new—when Sean first started taking the bus out of Simi Valley and going head first into the scene for shows in Hollywood. How very frightening and liberating it must have been at the time for her, but of course I think Sean De was way beyond the title "trendsetter"—the word for her is MOTHER, forever, for sure, and for always.

What is contained in the tiny pages of this book is a blaringly potent historical artifact of Black youth, seconds before their full realization into the scary world of adolescence and inevitable adulthood. Uncomfortable in parts? Yes, of course. I remember in eighth grade reading *The Diary of Anne Frank*—the uncensored version, which was withheld from the public until her father's death because he stated he could not live with the most private parts of his adolescent daughter's diary being consumed by the world. There is a certain sense of protection I feel for baby Sean De's most private thoughts being so exposed; however, so very little is written about the lives and the bold sexuality of young queers, and specifically young Black queers, that I also have to give regard that there is something ultimately explosive about this text. It also denotes the intense singularity of its author. A gay Black punk one generation AFTER DeLear, at the age of fourteen I was rather content staring at a wall and obsessing over my Lookout Records catalog—I can't even comprehend a gay Black kid some thirty years before planning to blackmail older white boys' dads for money for acting lessons. OK, like first of all, YAAAAAAAS BITCH, and second, this level of forward thinking is what propelled Sean De into becoming the scene girl to end all scene girls. I do have to imagine what level of this diary is real and what parts sit in an auto-fictional space—did she REALLY fuck all these old white dudes? Or was it a horny and advanced imagination at play? The only real answer is WHO CARES. I think one of the most magical things about Sean De was that her imagination and fantasy world was so absolute. The world she was spinning always BECAME true—this is the beauty of a shape shifter, and she was a noted scene darling and muse for this reason.

Now amidst all this magic of course was her fair share of trials and tribulations. Sean related to me that when her band Glue's music video for "Polara" debuted on MTV's *120 Minutes,* a higher-up in programming made a call to make sure that it was never shown again—and how sad.

Now, let's consider that Sean De's performance did not exist in a vacuum—I mean, if there was room for RuPaul, why not Sean De? Certainly, by the '90s there was room for a punk rock gender-defying Black child-gangster of the revolution—or then again, maybe not. Whereas RuPaul was relegated to the dance world, Sean De made rock and roll her drama—and rock and roll to this day REMAINS (disappointingly) the last stronghold of segregation in music. In a post-Afro-punk reality this should not be the case, but as desegregation proves itself to be a one-hundred-year period, Sean De's struggle to claim solidification and recognition in the world of SoCal '90s music comes as no real surprise. But also, as we are in an intense period of rediscovering buried histories and legacies, Sean De's is one of great note, triumph, and inspiration. As a matter of fucking fact, she is the Queen Mother of alternative music and in whatever higher realm of existence she is currently existing in, I can only imagine the sound of great explosions and bells ringing as she is gluing on her ICONIC eyelashes and receiving her flowers.

At the time of Sean De's death, I actually got a handful of her eyelashes, which I promptly put on my altar for the dead. I collected every zine she was in from the '90s, the Kid Congo record of which she was the subject, and lastly got to read and relish in the world of this great artist as a teen. I don't know how I got so lucky as to share a planet for a brief time with this punk rock fairy godmother, but you best believe that I pray to any god listening that I am grateful for such. Long live Sean DeLear.

Editor's Preface by Michael Bullock

To the Max

On September 5, 2017, I picked up a call. It was Cesar (Padilla); he was wailing in pain, unable to utter a single word. "Sh … Sh … Sea … Sean Deeee," he finally stuttered. "Sean Deeeee's dead." The news left me speechless. How was it possible? Sean DeLear seemed immortal to me. Larger than life. An energy. An idea. A muse who inspired so many boldfaced names. A walking work of art. A person who single-handedly made counterculture feel viable. His chosen name accurately reflected his flamboyant personality: bright and sparkling, like the chandeliers in the hotels and clubs that line Sunset Boulevard. To me, Sean DeLear was an important LA landmark, like the Hollywood sign. His life and art blurred lines between sexuality, gender, race, class, and genre. He was so many things: punk musician, intercontinental scenester, video vixen, dance-track vocalist, party host, heavy-metal groupie, marijuana farmer, and even Frances Bean Cobain's babysitter. If Sean DeLear sauntered into the party, you knew you were in the right place.

Today he would be called "nonbinary," although I think he would have never limited himself to this label. His look, like his art, was on his own terms. He was Sean DeLear uptown and downtown, crosstown and underground. His party attire gave starlet, as glamorous as a young Diana Ross. But most days he dressed somewhere in between—even his daytime "boy looks" low-key felt like drag. It was an effortless androgyny that included long fake eyelashes with a touch of bright lipstick on his big, beautiful lips, but worn with a ratty vintage band T-Shirt, a trucker cap, Nike high-tops, and striped athletic socks—fem on top, butch on bottom. His smile: enormous. His laugh: infectious. His presence: intoxicating. His voice: an original combination of sultry and baritone. When he spoke, he had a way of making you feel like you were being inner-circled into important secret histories, and his friendly, engaging personality and shape-shifting style allowed him to slip effortlessly between cultural scenes and systems.

As a result, Sean DeLear's illustrious biography includes both a cameo as Tone Loc's surprising date in the 1989 "Funky Cold Medina" video ("But when she got undressed, / it was a big old mess, / Sheena was a man"), and stints as a hostess at Johnny Depp's notorious LA club, the Viper Room. Later, in the '90s, he became a bona fide rock star as the lead singer of the seminal power pop–punk band Glue, gaining himself a list of unlikely celebrity fans, from Victoria Beckham to Yoko Ono to Trent Reznor (Glue opened for Nine Inch Nails). Lina Lecaro wrote in her 2017 *LA Weekly* obituary: "SeanD's lyrical and vocal tempestuousness won fans of all ilk—young, old, gay, straight, punk, alternative." In the 2000s, his romance with the art world advanced when he joined the Viennese collective Gelitin. He was also one of the only men to ever perform with Kembra Pfahler, as a backup dancer in her notorious art band the Voluptuous Horror of Karen Black. In the 2010s, he switched from punk to dance, collaborating with both Danish producer Jeppe Larsen (Junior Senior) and Filip "Turbotito" Nikolic of Ima Robot, on whose 2011 hit with Beni, "It's a Bubble," Sean was a vocalist. The lyrics are unmistakably Sean DeLear: "Hey streetwalker … You don't need to worry. I like the way you look. Your face is a mess, but hey we can fix you up."

Ultimately Sean DeLear didn't give a fuck about conventional success. What he cared about was looking good, having fun, being everywhere, and making art. In a tribute, friend Mike Hoffman (aka Surfer Mike) said that in Sean D's world there were "no such things as rules or shame." He did it all, with everyone, and he wore it well. A wild, original life without boundaries could sound messy, but Sean D pulled it off with an easygoing, happy-go-lucky elegance, and I always felt lucky for our friendship. Being in his presence expanded my understanding of personal freedom.

In 1979, the fourteen-year-old Sean wrote almost every day on everything: crushes, hustling, waterbeds, blackmail, the Village People, glory holes, racism, and shoplifting gay porn. His parents were one of the first Black couples to move to Simi Valley, a suburb of Los Angeles which in that period was well known for being racist. Members of Sean's immediate family were also extreme Christians. It is here that his nonconforming, sexually liberated existence developed the art of survival. Sean, who was already well versed in cruising, documented in his diary his attempts to sleep with as many dads as he could. Like a young Lolito, he dreamt about blackmailing them to pay for acting classes so he could become a Hollywood star (though he never actually went through with it). Reading this book, I realized something amazing: Sean D was not developed over time. He came into the world a fierce, fully formed faggot—or, to quote a famous song (produced by Jeppe Larsen), he was simply "born this way." Even Sean's evangelical parents were no match for his wild, glamorous, libidinous energy and I-don't-give-a-fuck confidence.

In the fun, fabulous pages of this rare, scandalous document, we are happy to share the personality and worldview of our friend who influenced so many people to live more courageously. Please enjoy this intimate window into the life of a boy who was never ashamed of his sexual attraction to other boys. Somehow, right from the start, against great odds, Sean DeLear always saw his sexuality as a great gift to be enjoyed, in the words of the diary, "to the max."

I Could Not Believe It: The 1979 Teenage Diaries of Sean DeLear

1979 CALENDAR

JAN

SUN	MON	TUE	WED	THU	FRI	SAT
	1	2	3	4	5	6
7	8	9	10	11	12	13
14	15	16	17	18	19	20
21	22	23	24	25	26	27
28	29	30	31			

FEB

SUN	MON	TUE	WED	THU	FRI	SAT
				1	2	3
4	5	6	7	8	9	10
11	12	13	14	15	16	17
18	19	20	21	22	23	24
25	26	27	28			

MAR

SUN	MON	TUE	WED	THU	FRI	SAT
				1	2	3
4	5	6	7	8	9	10
11	12	13	14	15	16	17
18	19	20	21	22	23	24
25	26	27	28	29	30	31

APR

SUN	MON	TUE	WED	THU	FRI	SAT
1	2	3	4	5	6	7
8	9	10	11	12	13	14
15	16	17	18	19	20	21
22	23	24	25	26	27	28
29	30					

MAY

SUN	MON	TUE	WED	THU	FRI	SAT
		1	2	3	4	5
6	7	8	9	10	11	12
13	14	15	16	17	18	19
20	21	22	23	24	25	26
27	28	29	30	31		

JUN

SUN	MON	TUE	WED	THU	FRI	SAT
					1	2
3	4	5	6	7	8	9
10	11	12	13	14	15	16
17	18	19	20	21	22	23
24	25	26	27	28	29	30

JUL

SUN	MON	TUE	WED	THU	FRI	SAT
1	2	3	4	5	6	7
8	9	10	11	12	13	14
15	16	17	18	19	20	21
22	23	24	25	26	27	28
29	30	31				

AUG

SUN	MON	TUE	WED	THU	FRI	SAT
			1	2	3	4
5	6	7	8	9	10	11
12	13	14	15	16	17	18
19	20	21	22	23	24	25
26	(27)	28	29	30	31	

SEP

SUN	MON	TUE	WED	THU	FRI	SAT
						1
2	3	4	5	6	7	8
9	10	11	12	13	14	15
16	17	18	19	20	21	22
23	24	25	26	27	28	29
30						

OCT

SUN	MON	TUE	WED	THU	FRI	SAT
	1	2	3	4	5	6
7	8	9	10	11	12	13
14	15	16	17	18	19	20
21	22	23	24	25	26	27
28	29	30	31			

NOV

SUN	MON	TUE	WED	THU	FRI	SAT
				1	2	3
4	5	6	7	8	9	10
11	12	13	14	15	16	17
18	19	20	21	22	23	24
25	26	27	28	29	30	

DEC

SUN	MON	TUE	WED	THU	FRI	SAT
						1
2	3	4	5	6	7	8
9	10	11	12	13	14	15
16	17	18	19	20	21	22
23	24	25	26	27	28	29
30	31					

This book belongs to
Tony Robertson — Please do
not read
because if I **1979**
find out I will
never talk to **DAILY**
you
REMINDER
again

& Mom or Dad
I will run a-
way for good, again
and THE STANDARD DIARY DIVISION
OF
ERIC WILSON JONES COMPANY

the
FUCKING **WJ**
ASS HOLE too!

MONDAY, 1 JANUARY 1979

Happy New Year Tony it is now midnight and one second. Well this is my first diary and I will write everything that happens to me in <u>1979</u>. Will write tonight Bye… Well I am going to bed now. So today there was a bitchen earthquake that was 4.6 on the Richter scale. Me and Terry went bowling today and me and Kim got in a fight on the phone. About Ken (fag-it) Kim still likes him even though he was going to ask her to go with him but he didn't. I thought of a name for you, Ty, short for Tyler, who works at the bowling alley and who I have a <u>crush</u> <u>on</u> <u>madly</u>. I don't know if he is gay or not but he is <u>so</u> <u>so</u> <u>so</u> <u>so</u> <u>cute</u> <u>cute</u>. Well I am going to go to bed now, so good night.

Love,
Tony

Dear Ty,

Today nothing happened. I went to school, worked in the middle of the MUR at lunch, and now I want to quit but I don't want to. I have to tell you about Bert & Ernie, my two pot plants. Bert is the one Barry gave me and Ernie is my plant he is so healthy I cannot believe it. I have to tell you about all my tricks…well there is Jack who gives the best blowjob, Jim who has the second best cum in Simi Valley, and Stewart who loves to stick his big cock up my ass. So I have a wide variety of tricks. I have to tell you about Tyler (hunk). He is about five foot nine or ten inches tall and has brown feathered hair, a hairy chest, and he wears his clothes unbuttoned down to his belly button, and he is so foxy with his tight pants. I want to see <u>his</u> <u>cock</u> <u>so</u> <u>bad</u>. Well that is all for tonight. Good night Ty.

Love,
Tony

WEDNESDAY, 3 JANUARY 1979

Dear Ty,

Today I went and saw the speaker and he was an actor. He said they have an actors' workshop and Mom said I could go, it costs $16.50 and she is going to pay for it too. Eric and Mom got in a fight today and he would not take out the Christmas stuff and now he is grounded for a <u>month</u>. When I watered Ernie today he almost got killed because I dumped water on him, but he is okay now. The rabbit Kim had gotten over Christmas got killed today by this dog. The dog bit Festise in the neck and broke it. Today I quit working at the MUR because GAIL IS SUCH A BITCH and I hate her guts but I am still going to get out of class early. Well that is about all for today. Good night Ty.

Love,
Tony

THURSDAY, 4 JANUARY 1979

Dear Ty,

Today I went to school and got a ton of homework from English. And I went to Gemco to see if they have a Loudmouth 8-track player but they don't. There was no one in the can as usual. I wish I could find a trick. If it was not so cold, I would go over the hill and see Jack and get some more books. I went to this actors' class and it was so fun. My teacher is Jimmy Daniel, he is so <u>cute</u>. I know he is not gay but I can dream. I wish I could get an agent so I could get some commercials. That would be so BITCHEN then I would make some real MONEY. I hope I do not fail English this quarter. If I do, I do not get any credits and that will be bunk. I want to send for *The David Kopay Story*...he is a gay football player, and get a book from the liquor store.

Love,
Tony

FRIDAY, 5 JANUARY 1979

Dear Ty,

My first week of school has gone by. Tomorrow I will bowl and I will tell you my scores and more about Tyler. It rained so hard today I had to do my papers in the car. It was hell. If it stops raining I am going to collect tomorrow. I have to pay my bill on time so I can get a pass to the show and one hundred points. I still don't know what I am going to get with all my points. I want that 8-track player so bad I would do anything just about. Tomorrow I have to go get my film from Thrifty. Well that is all for today.

Love,
Tony

SATURDAY, 6 JANUARY 1979

Dear Ty,

Today I went bowling. I bowled a 182 that is my high game. Tyler was so normal looking today I could not believe it. I did not know he was on the Simi High swim team. I hope he still is, I have to see him in a diving bathing suit. I hope it is so tight. I talked to Ken today but I am still mad at him. I went and got my film today, it cost $14.24 and I have to get one more roll still. I am going to go over the hill to see Jack on Monday. I hope he will want to suck me and I will suck him too. I have to find a trick I am so desperate. I'll go to the swap meet tomorrow and keep going in the john to find a trick. I want to suck some cock so bad. Sorry, I thought my mom was coming. Have to go to Gemco…I don't think I can go to Jack's, I don't know. If I get a trick I won't go.

Love,
Tony

SUNDAY, 7 JANUARY 1979

Dear Ty,

I went to the swap meet today, I did not find a trick anywhere but I saw some nick cock anyway. I got another Cheryl head, she is ugly. I got to cut her hair desperately. I am going to see Jack tomorrow. I am going to see Jack tomorrow. If it does not look like it will rain I will go, but I hope I don't get stuck in the rain over the hill. I ripped a *Hustler* from Simi Liquors today. It was so easy they were watching the Rams game on the portable TV. I want to get a lot of books at Jack's for my collection. I have to get the song "Fire." It is so good it's by the Pointer Sisters. It is the best song since "Evergreen." I want to be a singer and actor so bad I would kill to get a contract or movie or TV show. That would be so BITCHEN. Well, I am going to look at my *Hustler*. Good night.

Love,
Tony

MONDAY, 8 JANUARY 1979

Dear Ty,

I went to Jack's today. I sucked him till he came today. And I met this other guy. He had the nicest cock on him but he would not let me have his cum. He had never done it with a guy I think. He was so nervous I could not believe it. I got a *Blueboy*, *Honcho*, *Playgirl*, and *Hustler* rejects from Jack's store today. I wanted to get a *Numbers* or *Mandate* from the book stand but I could not, they got a lot of stuff, and they were putting it up. I cannot wait till I am sixteen so I can go to Santa Monica Blvd. Jack said that there are so many gays down there. I am going to put a new phone in my room tomorrow. I have to find out if Tyler is gay I will go look now if it is in the phone book… I could not find it, I will call the directory tomorrow. I love Tyler and want to get down with him.

Love,
Tony

TUESDAY, 9 JANUARY 1979

Dear Ty,

Nothing exciting happened today. I stole so much stuff today: first, two packs of Bubblicious, then two roles of 20-exposure film to take to school tomorrow, then two cans of vanilla frosting. What a thief. Kristy had a basketball game today and they won as usual. 38 to 12. We are undefeated so far and so was Hillside until today when we whipped them. I am going to go to Topanga Plaza on Friday. I think I hope it will be great if I pick somebody up over there. Well, it is late and I have to go to bed now. I will write a lot tomorrow OK.

Love,
Tony

WEDNESDAY, 10 JANUARY 1979

Kim's Birthday

Dear Ty,

I forgot all about Kim's birthday today. They had a cake for Gina the whore. I took my camera to school today and we had so much fun taking pictures all day. I want to get Pete's autowinder and take it to school tomorrow. I was on my way to Sav-on and Jim said that he lived right behind the school and he is Curtis's next door neighbor. I have to go over there tomorrow… no I can't I have acting class tomorrow. I will tell you about it. I cannot wait till I can suck Jim's cock this week or next week. I want that piece of meat up my ass so bad it will feel better than Stewart, he was so cute. But I will still love Tyler, I want to see his cock… I at least want to touch it. I would be happy.

Love,
Tony

THURSDAY, 11 JANUARY 1979

Dear Ty,

I went out tonight to this house up by school. But I did not see any cock or ass. I know he is gay but he would not let me come in. It was because he had his boyfriend over there and I don't think he wanted to do anything since I look so young. I have to become good friends with him. I know he is gay because he was looking at gay books with only naked guys in them but they hid them when I knocked. I gave all kinds of hints: I asked if there were any gay bars out here, used the phone book. I tried everything. I will go out tomorrow and tell you if I see any cock or get a mouthful I hope so. I will go watch wrestling tomorrow and take pictures. Well that is all I want to see Kim's dad's cock.

Love,
Tony

FRIDAY, 12 JANUARY 1979

Dear Ty,

Nothing happened today at school or anywhere else. I watched the rock awards tonight. Donna Summer won three awards. Her hair looked so bad I could not believe it. I think it was a wig. I am not going to go out tonight I am too fucking tired. I am going to go to bed now. I love Tyler he is so <u>cute</u>.

Love,
Tony

SATURDAY, 13 JANUARY 1979

Dear Ty,

I went to bowling today but I did not bowl so hot. You should have seen Tyler today, he got his hair cut and it looks so cute. It makes him look more like a girl. He has this cute friend; he has a nice piece of meat in his pants. Tyler is gay I am pretty sure. He has something wrong with his eye and was wearing glasses. He kept pulling them back like his hair was pinned back. I hope so I have such a crush on him. I went out and stayed out until 5:00 in the morning. I was laying down on some people's grass and the sprinklers came on by themselves. I thought it was raining, then I noticed it was the sprinklers, then I ran, then I noticed my watch on the ground. I ran and got my watch and then was hitchhiking to get some meat. No luck, then I went home. I am not going out until summer OK Ty. Good night or morning.

Love,
Tony

SUNDAY, 14 JANUARY 1979

Dear Ty,

Today it rained. I hate when it rains on the weekends. It ruins everything totally. I have to get the new *Playgirl*, it has the Village People in it and they are all gay, but one he's ugly though. Dad came over and we were going to go to the snow but that flopped. I made an angel food cake today and it came out so bitchen I could not believe it. I didn't do my papers until 8:30 this morning and I forgot my new house and they called and wanted a paper. I am going to make a date with Jim tomorrow, I will tell you when and all that

stuff. That is all for tonight, so good night. I Love TYLER. He is so
CUTE & a TOTAL BABE.

Love,
Tony

MONDAY, 15 JANUARY 1979

Dear Ty,

Well it rained all day long, I hate the rain so much. I was going
to go over to Jim's house today and make a date with him but it
rained. Did I ever tell you about me? Well, I am about five foot six
inches tall…I am Black, have a nice bod, am doing OK in school
except in English. My cock is about nine inches long and I love it.
I would love to pose nude for Jack, Jim, or Tyler and make a porn
film. My prize possession is a Minolta XG-7: my camera. It is
worth $250.00. I am gay, as you know I think. I have a lot of fan-
tasies about a lot of guys I know. When track starts, I will ask Burns
or Butts but not Mr. Detmer. I hate him. I always rip off things
from store mags and doll heads to cut their hair. I always seem to
have a hard-on I cannot believe it. When I am soft I am about four
inches long.

Love,
Tony

TUESDAY, 16 JANUARY 1979

Dear Ty,

I could not go to Jim's house today. I did not have any time at
all. I walked my papers today. I don't know why… Tomorrow I
am going on a field trip with my Cooking II class. It is late so I

have to write fast. I ripped off so much stuff today from Thrifty. I got this month's *Playgirl*, a new Jack, Neet hair remover for my ass and balls—I like my ass hairless—and two rolls of film. I am going to call Jack tomorrow at the store and get his home phone number so I don't always have to call before 4:00 p.m. at the store. I have to go to the house on the corner of Sequoia & Medina to find out if he wants to get it on with me. He has a nice cock I think. I have to write David tomorrow and find out where Tyler lives. Good night.

Love,

Tony

WEDNESDAY, 17 JANUARY 1979

Dear Ty,

Today was one hell of a day. We went on our field trip today, it was more fun than I thought it would be. We went to Lawry's Calif. Center where they make the stuff like seasoned salt. I talked to Jim today, he is going to call at 2:30 p.m. tomorrow. I am going to run home. Dad's grandma is in the hospital, they don't know what is wrong with her. They thought she had a stroke but she did not. I forgot to call Jack today, my bike tire popped and I was mad and I forgot. I am going to knock over the Skabbes' trash next week. We are not going to be here tomorrow night. I have acting class tomorrow and I know all of my lines. Well that is all. I love Tyler so much if we don't go to the snow Saturday I am going to ask him if he is gay and tell him that I love him. Good night.

Love,

Tony

THURSDAY, 18 JANUARY 1979

Dear Ty,

Jim called from work today and gave me his work number. He does not want me to call his home. We went to LA tonight to see Dad's grandma. It was so sad it made me sick to my stomach to see her. I hope she does not die until at least her 80th birthday or after. We stayed at Janise's tonight. I called to see how much it would cost to go to San Francisco; round trip it will cost $42.00. Then I would have to eat so that is $20.00 more. And to Santa Monica Blvd. it only costs 55 cents on RTD buses and to Dad's house it would cost $1.70 one way. That is not bad at all, I think it is cheap. Good night.

Love,
Tony

FRIDAY, 19 JANUARY 1979

Dear Ty,

Tonight we had our going away party for Wendy it was a lot of fun. The people who were there were Cindy, Gail, Lori, Kristi, Wendy, Mary, Alan, Roy, Bill, Gary, Aaron, and Doug. There were 14 people there and I had a ball. We played spin the bottle Alan kissed Wendy and she hated it because she is going to get married when she is out of school and she felt unfaithful to him. I like Mary, she is so cute I think she has a nice bod. We told Wendy we were going to Round Table Pizza for the party but it was at Cindy's house. The cake was chocolate so I did not eat any. I don't like chocolate at all. I am so COLD right now. Well Cupid and Arnold got out but we found Arnold but not Cupid. I hope she is alright. Please, dear God, don't kill her or Grandma. Good night.

Love,
Tony

SATURDAY, 20 JANUARY 1979

Dear Ty,

I found out Tyler's last name. I found out at bowling today. I did not bowl so hot today, I bowled a 125, 104, and a 120. My average is still 119, not too bad. I babysat Jay tonight and made $5.00, $1.00 an hour, not bad. On TV we watched *Heroes*. I am going to get up at 6:45 a.m. and do my papers then off to the swap meet tomorrow. I got Tyler's phone number if he still lives at home, it is 527-6439. I think I will go out one night next week it ain't so cold anymore. I will write David a letter tomorrow. I think I am going to bribe Jim for a lot of money but I don't know. I like him though. I am going to Jack's Thursday so Jack will take pictures of me in the <u>raw</u>. Good night.

Love,
Tony

SUNDAY, 21 JANUARY 1979

Dear Ty,

Nothing happened today. I went to the swap meet to meet a guy and get a trick but no luck as always. This one old man was looking at my cock and said "nice piece of meat," then I said "thank you," and that was it. I found out Tyler's phone number and he still lives there at home and now I have to find out if he is gay or not. That guy he hangs around with has a nice cock and is so cute just like Tyler. Well that is all for tonight. I still don't know if I will bribe Jim, if I do it will be about $500.00 or more. Good night. I love Tyler.

Love,
Tony

MONDAY, 22 JANUARY 1979

Dear Ty,

Today Grandma died. She was 78 and 204 ½ years old. I am sort of glad she died. She has been through hell all her life. I know I will miss her a lot but she is in heaven now. So she is better off in heaven than on earth half-dead. She died about 3:00 or 3:30 p.m. Mom said she told Katie she was coming and a bunch of other people that are dead already. She was so nice to us, I have five pictures of her that were taken around Christmas last year. Now Grandma is dead, I hope Cupid is not dead too. I hope she did not leave me anything because it would only remind me of her. I knew I would not cry when she died because she is better off where she is. Thank God. I will see you someday OK. Good night.

Love,
Tony

TUESDAY, 23 JANUARY 1979

Dear Ty,

Nothing happened to me. School was boring just like always. I want to get out of Calvi's class so bad I hate her guts so much. Today was the big game against Sequoia and Valley View. We lost our first game it was so depressing for us and the team and everyone else at the game. Valley View is undefeated now and we lost one. Tony P. filmed the first game on videocassette and we lost our first basketball game. The boy's team ain't so hot. Well that is all for tonight. I love Tyler.

Love,
Tony

WEDNESDAY, 24 JANUARY 1979

Dear Ty,

Today was the big banquet for our parents. It was a lot of fun for our parents and us. I hope tomorrow I have acting class and I hope I remember all of my lines or I will just die; and tomorrow is Wendy's last day at Sequoia. The guys had a basketball game today and we won 70 to 50-something I think. That is what Lupe told me. I saw Tracy L. today, what a hunk he is so cute. He let his hair grow long, what a babe he is. He gave me a weird look when I went by. Oh well, that is life. I will write David a letter tomorrow, and call Jim at work, and I will call Jack Friday or Saturday. I love Tyler so much it kills me. Good night.

Love,
Tony

THURSDAY, 25 JANUARY 1979

Dear Ty,

I got my first suit today. It is dark blue. I think it is so bitchen, I wore the pants, vest, and shirt to the dance. We went up on the stage and said "bye Wendy" it was so stupid I think we did not let the crowd calm down so they did not hear what we said at first. I had acting class today I remembered most of my lines better than some of the others. I will call Jim tomorrow and make plans for this weekend it will be fun I hope. I hope he is not busy this weekend like all the others. I will probably bribe him for the money. I could use that money so bad to get all the books and mags I want. Well tomorrow is the big day of sadness, I hope it is not that sad for anyone but I know it will be. Oh well. I love Tyler. Good night.

Love,
Tony

FRIDAY, 26 JANUARY 1979

Dear Ty,

Today was Grandma's funeral. She looked so good, like she was just asleep. It was a sad day for everyone. I got my hair done today and it will be so much easier to comb I hope. I will tell you tomorrow. I might get Grandma's piano, then I will take piano lessons and be like Elton John. I will sing, play the piano, and be GAY. I don't have much to say so I will say good night.

Love,
Tony

P.S. Bye Grandma.
I love you

SATURDAY, 27 JANUARY 1979

Dear Ty,

When I washed my hair it looked so bitchen. I wish it would stay that way but when it dries it looks like an Afro. I went to bowling today, we won three games and lost one. I bowled a 109, 81, and a 167. Not too bad, only me and Jerry were there. I could not believe it. Terry bowled good too. The other team was so dumb it was pitiful. Well I will tell you if I get the piano tomorrow when we go to LA. Good night.

Love,
Tony

SUNDAY, 28 JANUARY 1979

Dear Ty,

I get the piano for sure I cannot believe it. I am so happy I could just shit my pants. I will tell you when I get to start my lessons and when I get the piano. I have to call Jack, and Jim, and write David a letter. He does not know I got a camera for Christmas I don't think. I want to get a good job that will pay some money to pay for my piano lessons or become a ~~hooker or~~ hustler. It pays good money and I like to suck cock anyway. I got a canker sore on my lip and it hurts like a son of a bitch. I go to the doctor tomorrow. I think my teeth are going to fall out. I hope not, no more candy. Good night.

Love,
Tony

MONDAY, 29 JANUARY 1979

Dear Ty,

I get the piano tomorrow at 8:00. How bitchen. I hope this silver oxide stuff is off my lip by tomorrow. Jim called and wanted me to come over to his house because no one was home at his house but I could not go, I wish I could have but that is life. I will call tomorrow. I will call Jack Wednesday and get his home phone number then on Sunday I can go over to his house or in his car. I want to do it in the back seat of his car just for fun. Why not? I still have not wrote David a letter. I will try to do it this week sometime. Good night. I LOVE TYLER the total <u>babe</u>.

Love,
Tony

TUESDAY, 30 JANUARY 1979

Dear Ty,

I was right, Wood was full so it looked like I would have to stay in Metal, but I can get my whole schedule changed and PE first. Then I could see Victor's cock and Mark, Dale, Ryan, and that new guy who hangs around with Mark. Instead of Metal, I will have Office Practice and I will answer the phone, run passes, and file which I hate. Oh well. I did not get the piano because it rained and it is an open truck that they would bring it on so I hope it stops raining soon so I have my piano. I cannot wait till I get it. Well that is all for now. Good night.

Love,
Tony

WEDNESDAY, 31 JANUARY 1979

Dear Ty,

My papers were two hours late can you believe it, they got here at 6:30. The printing press broke down so they had to fix it. Oh well. I will wash my hair tomorrow and see what happens to it. I get my classes changed tomorrow. I will have Office Practice, how bitchen, but most of all I will have PE first offering and I will see Victor, Dale, Mark, Ryan, and that new guy's cock, how BITCHEN. I wish I could take pictures of them showering it would be so radical but I can't. I can't wait till track starts I hope I will win a lot of races. I have faith in myself. I will go to Simi High School and watch them shower I hope—or some other high school. I will tell you about it tomorrow. Good night.

Love,
Tony

THURSDAY, 1 FEBRUARY 1979

Dear Ty,

Well I did not get my schedule changed yet but I have to be at school by 8:00 or 8:15 to get it changed. Now I have PE first and I get to see all new cock meat. Victor's & Mark's & Dale's most of all. I had acting class today at the Larwin Community Center. I remembered most of my lines. I will tell you about my Simi High fantasy tomorrow. I might try out for *Bye Bye Birdie*, a play at the Horizon Players workshop. We have to sing a song. I hope I make it. Now I need a song to sing. If it does not rain tomorrow I will call Jack and Jim and just talk to Jack and try to get a date with Jim. I hope it works out for the weekend. Good night.

Love,
Tony

FRIDAY, 2 FEBRUARY 1979

Dear Ty,

Well, it rained all day today so I could not call Jack or Jim so now I won't make it over there this weekend I don't think. Well, I got my schedule changed and I can't wait to see all that fat cock in PE. I have bowling tomorrow and I will tell you my scores. I hope I do good. My Simi High fantasy is to go up to the school and go in the locker room and hope I see some cock. Which, I will for sure or I will go to that school over the hill by where the Simi bus drops me off and walk down the street to the school and if I get caught they won't know me. It will be so bitchen when and if it stops raining soon. I hope they are having a track tournament at school and I plan on winning a lot of events just like at Sycamore. Good night Ty.

Love,
Tony

SATURDAY, 3 FEBRUARY 1979

Dear Ty,

I went to bowling today and bowled a 135, 127, and 114. Not bad. Tyler's friend is not gay; this girl was climbing all over him. Oh well. We got a new coach at bowling. He is sort of cute and sort of ugly but he has a nice cock and he does not try to hide it either. He went into the bathroom, went to the end one and stood about a foot and a half away from the john and saw me looking and did not move an inch still. It is about seven or eight inches long. I could take the whole thing if he let me. And he went twice and so did I and he stood at the same place. I am going to go to the swap meet tomorrow if we don't go to the snow. I want to go to both but it will be one or the other. Good night.

Love,
Tony

SUNDAY, 4 FEBRUARY 1979

Dear Ty,

Today we went to the snow. It was so bitchen. We only had one saucer but it was still fun. There was this big drop-off and me and Terry almost threw each other off the edge. Dad was pissed off because I would not give him the other half of my lemon pie so I got out of the car and went back up the mountain and that was that. I want to go back next week but I don't think we will be able to. If we get to go back I will have an inner tube by then I hope. Well that is all for tonight. I still love Tyler. Good night.

Love,
Tony

MONDAY, 5 FEBRUARY 1979

Dear Ty,

Today I went to donkey basketball it was so much fun I had a ball. The teachers won by two points in overtime. Tracy was there, he is so cute I would love to have his cock down my throat and taste his hot white <u>cum</u>. I would love to taste anyone's <u>cum</u> for that matter. My Donna Summer, *Live and More* tape came today. I am listening to it right now. "Last Dance" is on now. I have a track meet tomorrow and I plan on winning a lot of events. I will tell you what I <u>win</u> tomorrow. Well it is late so I have to get my rest so I can win all the events tomorrow.

Good night.

Love,

Tony

TUESDAY, 6 FEBRUARY 1979

Dear Ty,

Today we had track races and my times were 11.2 and 11.3 and I got 2nd place by one second in both races. Oh well. I still don't have my bill for my papers. I will call Jack and Jim tomorrow. I don't have PE so I don't get to see any cock. Oh I did see some: Bob's and some other kid's. Bob has a nice one and a lot of hair and that other kid had a pointer with a lot of foreskin on his cock. Well that is all for tonight I think. Yep. Good Night. I still love TYLER and I want to see his cock so bad. Good Night again.

Love,

Tony

WEDNESDAY, 7 FEBRUARY 1979

Dear Ty,

I called Jack and he was not there and I called Jim and he was already home so better luck next time. I was going to go to Jack's tomorrow but I can't because Mom is going over the hill to get the car fixed. I have acting class tomorrow. I wish I could go over the hill. I ripped off a *Hustler* and some other fuck magazine and I put them between the fence and the next door neighbor found them. The *Hustler* has "Rocky" Sylvester Stallone in the nude…he has the littlest dick and in another photo spread this guy has the longest rod in the world, about nine or ten inches long. Well, Good Night.

Love,
Tony

THURSDAY, 8 FEBRUARY 1979

Dear Ty,

Today I did the long jump and got almost 15 feet, not bad. I had acting class today and I think the play will be okay. I hope I don't forget my lines and my cues. Well if I forget, oh well—there is nothing I can do about it. Tomorrow I am going to go to Topanga Plaza and try to get a trick and if I do I will swipe all his money, or her money. And Chatsworth High is right across the street and I will go into the locker room and act like I am looking for someone and I will say I am from Great Falls, Montana. I am looking for David. I hope I get some money or I might just rob a store for all you know. But I don't think so. Good night.

Love,
Tony

FRIDAY, 9 FEBRUARY 1979

Dear Ty,

Well I went to Topanga Plaza and was in the tearoom and stuck my cock out to this man and he was a cop and he arrested me for masturbating in a public restroom. Can you believe it? They took me to the police station handcuffed then they called my mom and she had to come get me. She asked me if I thought I was gay and I told her I don't know. I went to the high school and could not find the locker room and there were a lot of hunks. Then at about 2:30 a.m. I got my mom's keys to the Zee and went for a little bit of a spin. It was so bitchen at first. I almost hit a car and from then on I was very careful. I went about 25 miles. I went to Simi Bowl and there was no one and then over the hill to Rocket Bowl and they were not open. I came home and Mom went through my room and called Dad.

Love,

Tony.

SATURDAY, 10 FEBRUARY 1979

Dear Ty,

In the morning Dad was here and he gave me a lecture about why I went over the hill and for what. I don't know how to tell them that I think I am gay. I don't think I will tell them at all. I had so much fun driving last night. Dad said, "You don't know how to drive." That is what he thinks. Oh well. I went to bowling today and I was the only one there and we won two games. I bowled a 115, 149, and a 169, not bad. I did not go in the tearoom that much because of yesterday over the hill. But I did see this one man's cock—not bad, about six and a half inches long, not that thick at all. Well tomorrow is the big day, I hope I can spin the basketball on my finger and don't drop it. I hope it will be fun. I wonder how long I will be grounded for ditching and taking the car. When I find out I will tell you. This will be the first time this year. Good night.

Love,

Tony

SUNDAY, 11 FEBRUARY 1979

Dear Ty,

Well today was the big day of the play and it was OK and I didn't drop the basketball when I spun it on my finger. I remembered all my lines I was so glad. Mom did not take my mags away from me that she found Friday night so I put them back where they belong and nobody knows where they are. We have a three-day weekend but I have four days. I am going to build a fishpond I started digging today and it is half dug up. I want to get little turtles and goldfish and all kinds of plants around it. I hope it does not cost a lot of money. I might get my phone put in but I don't know. I wonder when I get Grandma's piano I want to get it so I can learn to play <u>super good</u>. Good night.

Love,

Tony

MONDAY, 12 FEBRUARY 1979

Dear Ty,

Well I finished my fishpond, now all I have to do is get some cement and fish and turtles and a lot of plants to go all around it. I just thought of something—I have to get a good filter to keep it clean so I don't have to clean it every day. I want to get a good one. I still don't know when I get to be a free man again. I will probably be grounded for a week or two. I hope it is not long for my sake. It will be a long time I know her too well to let me off that easy. I meant to ask about the piano but I forgot again. I don't think it will be too soon, don't you worry. I still love <u>Tyler</u> he is a total babe so is <u>Dale</u> and <u>Victor</u>. I want their COCKS.

Love,
Tony

TUESDAY, 13 FEBRUARY 1979

Dear Ty,

It started to rain today so I can't do my pond today. I don't think it will ever be finished but I can hope and pray. Today I was at Santa Susana Liquors and this old lady was looking at the naked ladies in the mags I could not believe it. She was probably a lez so who cares anyway. Then I went to Simi Liquors and they have the new *Playgirl* and the centerfold is a total fox with a huge cock and nice balls. I still don't know when I will be a free gay person again. Probably a month or so; I hope not. I have to find out where Victor and Dale live so I can see them masturbate alone or together. I hope they do it together. If they do it together I will join them and spread it all over school and that will be hell for those two forever… Good night.

Love,
Tony

WEDNESDAY, 14 FEBRUARY 1979

Dear Ty,

In office practice I did not get a chance to find out where Dale and Victor live. Well I went to McDonald's for lunch and brought it back to school for me and Kim. Everybody was pissed off at me for not getting them something to eat. Oh well. Tomorrow we have our first big test in Mr. Billing's class. I hope I get a good grade, better than Michelle's. I still don't know when I get to be a free gay person again. Right now, I am laying on my big nine-inch cock with a full erection—wish Dale's cock was up my ass right now but no POSSIBLE WAY. Or Victor's in my mouth so bad. I still don't know when I get the piano. Max and Glenda think I broke into their house last night but I didn't and I know that for sure so they can FUCK OFF. Good night.

Love,

Tony

THURSDAY, 15 FEBRUARY 1979

Dear Ty,

Nothing at all happened today. I still don't know when I get the piano. Well, that's all for tonight. I still love Tyler and want to see Dale's, Victor's, and Ryan's cocks so bad. I want to find out where Victor and Dale live. Well, good night.

Love,

Tony

FRIDAY, 16 FEBRUARY 1979

Dear Ty,

It has been one week since I got picked up by the pigs in the bathroom, and one week since I drove the car at night, and one week since I have been grounded. I still don't know how long I am grounded. I think I will quit my paper route. I am so sick of Mr. Drunk, I am ready to just quit at the end of the month. I got Victor's and Dale's address. I can't find either street so I have to get a map of Simi Valley. Well, good night.

Love,
Tony

TUESDAY, 27 FEBRUARY 1979

Dear Ty,

I am sorry I have not written in a week or so but nothing happened at all! Well, I have decided I don't want my route so Lori will do it tomorrow and for all of March. I know what I will get Mom for her birthday…this ring she wants. Me, Eric, and Dad will split the cost three ways I hope. Tomorrow I have to go talk to someone about what happened last Friday in the tearoom. Mom found some of my mags but did not say a word about them, I wonder why. Maybe she put them back, I will see tomorrow. On the first is Michelle's birthday and I will make a cake for her to eat at lunch and we will have a little party for her. Well that is all for today. I love Tyler & DALE (what a babe). Good night.

Love,
Tony

WEDNESDAY, 28 FEBRUARY 1979

Dear Ty,

Today I made Michelle's cake. It is a white cake with white frosting and blue writing and trim. I hope I did not cook it too long. Well I am ready to cement my pond, I will put foil on the bottom instead of chicken wire. I will take my camera to school tomorrow and take pictures at the party. Lori did my route today and I enjoyed not doing it so much. I might get to like it but I might just quit but I doubt it because I need the money. I forgot to look and see if I put the mags back. I hope so. I don't think Dale or Victor shower in PE so I may never get to see their cocks after all but I want to so bad. I don't like Tyler so much but I won't change your name from Ty, I promise. Good night.

Love,
Tony

THURSDAY, 1 MARCH 1979

Dear Ty,

It was so sunny yesterday and it rained today, it even hailed; so there was no track today—we got out sweatsuits today and they are not that old looking. Today I got the March *Playgirl*. Well, I took my camera to school today to take pictures of Michelle's cake and stuff like that and she was being a bitch (like always) because she left the rollers in her hair for too long and it looked tweeked. This month's centerfold is so bitchen. He has the nicest looking cock in the world. I did not have the chance to look if Mom found my mags or not. I don't think so or she would have said something by now I think. I will look for sure tomorrow sometime I hope. Well, good night.

Love,
Tony

FRIDAY, 2 MARCH 1979

Dear Ty,

Well I looked and they are all gone and she has not said anything, I wonder why. Me and her are in a fight and this morning I walked out, did not say bye, did not eat—just walked out. In the *Playgirl* I just got, there are these two guys who have hard-ons and another guy who I can't tell. Well it is sunny out today. This weather is so weird I can't believe it. Mom went on this trip to Frazier Park I hope she gets killed. She is being such a bitch. So Dad is here right now and he said if I go out he will break my neck. I won't, I am too tired. Well, good night.

Love,
Tony

SATURDAY, 3 MARCH 1979

Dear Ty,

I went to bowling today and we won all four games. I bowled a 143, 115, and a 143, not bad…I hope my average goes up. We are at Dad's house right now; I went out tonight. It was a total dud, but one thing I liked was there were a lot of cars and people out on the streets, not like in Simi. I was walking home and I met this guy but he was not gay, I asked him and he did not get mad because he was higher than the clouds on coke. But other than him it was a dud. They fixed the hole in the wall at the bowling alley by putting a piece of metal over the hole and welding it. Well, good night.

Love,
Tony

SUNDAY, 4 MARCH 1979

Dear Ty,

Well I am back at home now and I could not get any mags like *Blueboy, Numbers, Honcho* or *In Touch for Men* but that's okay. I will get them somehow. Tomorrow we go to the probation officer to see what he wants to do with me. He won't do anything just like all the rest of them. What a bunch of <u>suckers</u>. I wonder how much longer I will be grounded for. It has been a month on Friday. I will ask Mom tomorrow. I wonder when I get the piano too? Oh well. I went collecting today and I made about $50 this month, what a surprise. I did not spend all my money like always. Well Good night Ty. I love you.

Love,
Tony

MONDAY, 5 MARCH 1979

Dear Ty,

I finished collecting today and I think Mark J. is gay. He is always in his room. If he is in school he must study a lot but that is still a lot of studying. I have to ask him one day if he is gay, if I get the nerve which I doubt I will. Well we went to court today and I have to go to counseling again. See, they did not do nothing like I said. I forgot to ask Mom how much longer I am grounded, I have to ask tomorrow. I hope Mark is gay, he is such a cutie I cannot believe it. Now I have a crush on (in order) Dale, Tyler, Mark, and Victor. I love them all anyway. Good night.

Love,
Tony

TUESDAY, 6 MARCH 1979

Dear Ty,

If you are wondering where my other pen is, it got left at school by mistake...I will bring it home tomorrow if I remember. I was going to go to track this morning but I was too late so I just went after school. Well I got in another fight with Mom about her ignoring me all the time. I want to move out of this prison. She makes me so mad that I took all my posters down, took the stuff off my shelves, and there is nothing on the walls or on my dressers or on my shelves. I want to move out so bad, I would kill for it if I had to. She makes me so <u>MAD</u> that <u>FUCKEN BITCH</u>, and I hope you read this you <u>scum</u> and a <u>bitch</u>. Good night.

Love,
Tony

WEDNESDAY, 7 MARCH 1979

Dear Ty,

Well I forgot my pen again, I am so sick of it anyway. Well I am talking to Mom again I don't know why. I went to track this morning and was late, I ain't going no more. I took my coupons to school today and was going to go cash them after school but they got ripped off and so did my book *The Exorcist* and I was on a good part in the book. Well that is all for tonight. Well, good night.

Love,
Tony

THURSDAY, 8 MARCH 1979

Dear Ty,

I forgot my pen today. I think it got ripped off at school. I got my coupons and my book back. Guess who had them—Kenny, he sits next to me in English and that is why I could not find it (pen). It figures, he had it…I did not think I lost it because I have been carrying it around for weeks and have not lost it. I did not go to track today in the morning or after school. I went and cashed all my points in...and I know where Dale gets off the bus now and the fastest way to his house. Oh well. I still think Mark is a cutie and I would love that rod of his down my mouth and his cum. He would like it too I think. Good night.

Love,
Tony

FRIDAY, 9 MARCH 1979

Dear Ty,

Well Monday I have to go to track in the morning or I am off the team for good. Oh well. We got our progress reports today and I got a D in Oceanography. I am going to fail I think, I hope not. That class is so hard, he gives us so much FUCKEN homework I can't believe it. Every night homework and I never do it so I will probably get an F for the quarter. I am babysitting right now, they pay about five dollars or so. I might ask Kristy to the formal on the 7th of April. I don't know if she is going or not, we will have to wait and see. Good night.

Love,
Tony

SATURDAY, 10 MARCH 1979

Dear Ty,

Well today I went to bowling and I bowled so bad two games. One game was 148, the others were 103 and a 113, not so good. I don't think we won one game anyway. Well tomorrow is Mom's birthday. I went to bowling by hitchhiking a school teacher from Royal High School and he drove me right to the front steps of the bowling alley. That was nice of him. His son was in the car too…he was sort of cute from my view. I didn't just turn and stare at him, he would have thought I was weird or something. Oh well. I got five dollars for watching Jay last night. Today was his birthday and tomorrow is Mom's—she will be 39 ha ha!

Good night.

Love,

Tony

SUNDAY, 11 MARCH 1979

Bitch's

Mom's Birthday

Dear Ty,

Well guess what, Dad wants to put the house up for sale. I am so glad we can list with Kim's mom and I will get my $100.00 commission for the listing with her. How bitchen. Well I have to bury my pond, thank God. I have no cement or anything else. Mom is going to live out here in Simi I hope. Me and Eric are going to live with Dad. How bitchen. I can't wait till we get out of this dump. I want to move so bad, this is a dream come true! I don't think Mom wants to move, tough luck BITCH. I got Mom a rose and Eric got her a stickpin with a diamond in the middle of a butterfly and we got her a cake. She is a big 39 years old. Good Night.

Love,

Tony

MONDAY, 12 MARCH 1979

Dear Ty,

Well I went to school today and nothing exciting happened at all. Dad wants to sell the house through Pete, then I won't get the $100.00. That gets me <u>pissed</u>. Pete does not even work out in Simi so he can't sell it anyway I don't think. I think they should sell the house for no less than $100,000.00 at least. I wonder how much the realtor and Uncle Sam get out of it. "Oh Well" (my new word). Lorainne had her baby today. It's a little boy. Now Marlie has a little brother and we have a baby cousin on Mom's side of the family. I hope we list with Kim's mom so I can get the money, I need it. Well that's all. Oh, I forgot, I get my phone put in as soon as I can, <u>bitchen</u>. Good night.

Love,

Tony

TUESDAY, 13 MARCH 1979

Dear Ty,

Well I got my pen back. It did not get ripped off like I thought. I went to Gemco to get a phone jack and they don't have them. School was a total dud like always. I don't know how long I am grounded for yet. I hope not much longer. I wonder when I get the piano. I hope soon. I want it so bad. Well that is all for tonight. Good Night.

Love,

Tony

THURSDAY, 15 MARCH 1979

Dear Ty,

We had our first track meet today but it got rained out. Our next meet is on Thursday the 22nd. I don't know where though. Tomorrow I have to go to the shrink with Dad and find out what happens about the tearoom incident. I don't think anything will happen at all, I hope not. TOMORROW IS THE DANCE and I will go like always and just stand around like always. It is raining hard now. No track in the morning. Oh, I got my portable AM-FM-8-track player. It cost $48.00 from Volume, not bad huh. Well good night.

Love,
Tony

FRIDAY, 16 MARCH 1979

Dear Ty,

Well we went to the shrink today and he is going to put me on unofficial probation for a while till I get my act together. I went to the dance tonight and it was so much fun. There were not a lot of people there and I had a good time. I forgot to tell Mr. Detmer or Mr. Fergeson I would not be at track. I hope I do not get in trouble and then I won't be able to jump at the meet on the 22nd. I will just die. Well good night.

Love,
Tony

SATURDAY, 17 MARCH 1979

St. Patrick's Day

Dear Ty,

Went bowling today and bowled a 121, a 126, and a 141. Not bad for an amateur. Well, I started to fill in my pond by putting the dirt back in. It was easier than taking it out. Well it stopped raining today, it was sunny all day long. At the bowling alley there was this guy sitting on the can the whole time we were there and Terry told me when we were ready to leave, I was so pissed off that made me mad. I could have gotten some cock and cum down my mouth. Oh well, that's the breaks. Well good night.

Love,

Tony

SUNDAY, 18 MARCH 1979

Dear Ty,

Well I can't find my pen again. Today everything happened to me. First, Kim finally came and got my hamster cage. Then it was sunny so me and Terry were going to go swimming today but then it started to hail…then rain…then there was nothing to do the rest of the day. Then Eric had told me about the party line. It was so bitchen. When you talk you hear people but you can only hear them when this recording goes off. That what is so bad about it, but I got a whole list of numbers. I told Kim, Lori, and Kristy it is so neat. I wonder if there is a real party line, I doubt it. "Oh well." Good night.

Love,

Tony

MONDAY, 19 MARCH 1979

Dear Ty,

Well it rained today like all last week. Mom got pissed that we are on the party line. Well she can fuck off. I had a test in Billing's class today. I hope I get a good grade on it, I studied a little but not much. Nothing happened that exciting at all. Oh, I forgot, I went to Santa Sue liquors today and got a *His & Hers* mag and a new book (paperback) to read. It's called *Cop Out*. It is OK so far. It is better than *Young Men of the Night*. There is more action in *Cop Out*. Well that's all. Good night.

Love,
Tony

TUESDAY, 20 MARCH 1979

Dear Ty,

Well I got a C on my test in Billing's class. Well me, Mom, and Eric got in the biggest fight of them all. I was so mad I called Dad and asked if when we move he (Eric) can stay in Simi with Mom so that BITCH and that ASSHOLE can stay away from me, so me and Dad can live happily ever after. "Oh Well." I want to ditch tomorrow and go over the hill. I don't know if I will yet. I want to but we have a meet Thursday after school and I don't think I should risk it again. But I want to get it on with someone. I got a *His & Hers* and there is this ad for a bodybuilder maybe he will want to get it on, you never know. I want to have an affair anyway. I am going to write a suicide note and let Mom find it (ha ha). Well, Good Night.

Love,
Tony

WEDNESDAY, 21 MARCH 1979

Dear Ty,

Today I ditched school to go see Jack. I did not get caught. Me and Jack were in the store necking and holding each other. It felt so good. Then someone came in, and he works there, so that was that. He has a lover that lives with him so he can't take me home. He said come back next Wednesday and we would have a hot sucking and necking time. I got two new mags: a *Honcho* and a *Blueboy*. They are both pretty gnarly and I went to the book stand and just started looking at the gay mags and the guy who works there said to tell him which one I wanted and he would put it in a bag and I could read it at home, I didn't have any money. There is the new mag that costs $8.75 but it is worth it all the way because it has a lot of hard-ons all through it. I wanted to rip it off. "Oh well." Well I might ditch tomorrow I don't know. Oh, I have to write a "suicide note." Well good night.

Love,
Tony

THURSDAY, 22 MARCH 1979

Dear Ty,

Well I only went to school the last five minutes so I could go to the meet. I went and it was a total dud and three quarters. Well I went to Coast Valley Spas & Racquetball today it was so bitchen. I said Dad was a member and I was 16 years old. I might go on Saturday if I can and have enough time to. Well when I went back to school I got caught. Someone saw me on Devonshire yesterday, what a bust. I hope not. Well that is all for tonight. Good night.

Love,
Tony

FRIDAY, 23 MARCH 1979

Dear Ty,

Well you will never guess what I did to Terry? Mom went to a basketball game in LA tonight and I spent the night at Terry's house. First we started play-fighting and he was winning until I grabbed his cock and it was hard as a brick wall. Well, I was already hard anyway because I am gay that's why I grabbed at his cock. Then we stopped and went to bed, then we started talking about sucking cock and I said "I would" if he put it in my mouth. He had to make the first move. Then he did. I put my head back on the bed and he stood up and put it in my mouth. His cock has gotten a lot bigger than it was. Then I started sucking hard on it, then he shot his cum all over my mouth but pulled away too fast and cummed on my chest and that was the end of that. Hope we do it again. Good night.

Love,
Tony

SATURDAY, 24 MARCH 1979

Dear Ty,

Well I went to Coast Valley Spa & Raquetball today it was so fun. First, I did these exercises they told me to do for my legs for track. They think I am going to really join the club but that is a bunch of bull anyway. Then off to the pool, there it was a lot of fun. I saw so many cocks and I had a hard-on the whole time I was in the pool. There was this one guy with the most BITCHEN BOD and we were in the vapor room and I of course had a hard-on and he was laying down on his back and had his eyes closed and I was just staring right at his cock it was not all that big but it was nice and he had a semi hard-on. Oh well. I want to go back on the weekend. I hope. Well I went bowling today too. I bowled a 178, 131, and 105, not bad. I brought my average up I hope. I don't like Tyler anymore. "Oh well"! Well good night.

Love,
Tony

SUNDAY, 25 MARCH 1979

Dear Ty,

Well today we had to cut the grass good so we can show the house as soon as possible. Well I borrowed Pete's 200 mm zoom lens for my camera today to take pictures of my hamster's face. Now I can't wait to get them back to show off to everyone at school. Well I have to take my radio back because the 8-track player plays the tapes too slow in the machine. So I am going to get my money back and save my money for a waterbed, or an autowinder, or a tripod, or a good, good remote control car like at Smith Brothers' hobby store. Who knows what. Well good night.

Love,
Tony

MONDAY, 26 MARCH 1979

Dear Ty,

Well I went to school today and nothing at all happened. I forgot all about the extra-credit assignment due in Oceanography today. I would have done it at lunch but I did not have enough time and I had it first anyway. Well I finished my roll of film with the 200 mm zoom lens today. I will take the pictures in as soon as possible. Mom did not take back my radio today, she said. Maybe tomorrow I hope, I don't like it all that much anyway. Well, good night.

Love,

Tony

TUESDAY, 27 MARCH 1979

Dear Ty,

Well I might quit track. I don't know yet, I probably will though. Well I got another roll of film today and I forgot that there are 36 pictures on a roll and when I got to 20 I rewound the film and then I realized that it was 36 exposures. I don't think I will be able to use the pictures anyways. I was going to see Jack tomorrow but I am not since I got caught last time and it is raining anyway. Well that's all for tonight. Good night.

Love,

Tony

WEDNESDAY, 28 MARCH 1979

Dear Ty,

Well I did not go to Jack's today but I wished I would have. I love him so much I think. Well I want to get it on with him anyway. Well I did not go to track today so I guess that means I quit. Well it rained again only at night not during the day I am so glad. I hate the rain so much I like the snow better. Mom took my radio back today and I got my $47.67 back. I want some more mags so bad. Maybe I will go rip off one. Who knows. "Oh Well." Good night.

Love,

Tony

THURSDAY, 29 MARCH 1979

Dear Ty,

Nothing happened today at all. Well tomorrow is the end of the quarter. "Oh Well." I don't think my grades are going to be so good this quarter. "Oh Well." Well I don't know what the hell I am going to do with my money. I never do know what I am going to do with it anyway. "Oh Well." Well that's all for tonight. Good night.

Love,
Tony

FRIDAY, 30 MARCH 1979

Dear Ty,

Well I took my camera to school today and we took a lot of pictures. Well I quit track today, it was getting so boring anyway. Well I stayed up to watch the *Midnight Special* and the Village People were on the show and that construction worker is a total babe and three quarters. Well I have to fix my bike tomorrow because I want my paper route on Sunday. What a dud. Well I have bowling tomorrow, I will tell about it tomorrow. Well good night.

Love,
Tony

P.S. The construction worker has the nicest cock I have ever seen through jeans.

Love,
Tony

SATURDAY, 31 MARCH 1979

Dear Ty,

Well I went to bowling today and guess what happened? Tyler is gay or bi I don't know yet. Well this is what happened. First I went to the bowling alley at about 1:00 and I did not wear underwear so I could get a trick, well it worked! I kept going in the bathroom and Tyler followed me in but did not do anything so I was beginning to think twice but I did not give up. (There was this other guy and he was my height and had a nice bod but did not try anything.) Then Tyler was sitting down, so was I; and they put this piece of metal over the cock hole in the wall but you could still see through and there was toilet paper stuffed in the hole and I pulled it out (daring). Then I could see him and he would not let me see his cock, then he did. It is bigger than mine I just flipped out. Then he bent down and I SUCKED his cock and I know he is gay because he was giving me a hand job. Then someone wanted him at the desk and they came in the tearoom. Well I called tonight but his number is busy and I keep trying but it is still busy. Good night.

Love,
Tony

SUNDAY, 1 APRIL 1979

Dear Ty,

This must be my luckiest weekend. Yesterday with Tyler and today this guy I met at the swap meet. First I went into the can and I saw some nice cocks. There was this one guy who had suck-tight pants you could see every bump and bulge in his jeans. He had a cock about 5" to 6" long soft. Well, the guy I met today had a nice big cock and we left the swap meet and went out in a field and made out. It felt so good I want to go down there every weekend even though I won't be able to. His cock was about 8" long and his foreskin covered the whole head I could not believe it. It turned me on so much, his cum tasted so bad though. He was a little taller than me and probably about in his late 30s but he was nice. But he lives out in LA and comes all the way out to the Simi Swap Meet to get head. That is a long way for head. "Oh Well." I did not have the nerve to call Tyler today. I will wait till Sat. and talk then. <u>Good</u> <u>luck</u> I hope. Well that's all for tonight. Good night. Sweet dreams about Tyler.

Love,

Tony

MONDAY, 2 APRIL 1979

Dear Ty,

Well nothing at all happened today at school. I went to a track meet after school today and found Wendy in that great big school can you believe it. "Oh Well." I went into the guy's locker room it is so big. I bet after gym there are so many nice cocks in the showers and I saw the coach of Valley View Jr. High's cock. It was super thick but not that long. "Oh Well." I did not have sex today, oh too bad, I wish I could have. Well good night.

Love,

Tony

TUESDAY, 3 APRIL 1979

Dear Ty,

Well guess what I found out today. We get report cards Friday then people will be grounded all Easter week, what a dud huh. Well tomorrow are the tryouts for the $1.98 beauty contest. I hope it will be fun and I hope a lot of people show up for the contest. If a lot of people show up it will be so much fun. But if they don't it will be a total dud—well that's the breaks if nobody shows up. They will be too embarrassed to show up. Anyway that's what they will say. Well that's all, good night.

Love,
Tony

WEDNESDAY, 4 APRIL 1979

Dear Ty,

Well the band was in the MUR today after school so we could not have the tryouts. No one showed up anyway except Patty and there was drill team after school and a track meet so any girl who would have tried out either had drill team or track and there was a gymnastics meet after school today anyway. Well that's all for tonight. Good night.

Love,
Tony

THURSDAY, 5 APRIL 1979

Dear Ty,

Tomorrow I am going to go to Jack's and be back by 2:30 to get my report card and if I miss the bus I will just die. I have to get over there before 11:00 because someone else works there and that's the time they come in and I have to be at school by 7:45 to take a test in Oceanography or else take the make-up test and it's a lot harder than the first one. I hope I get a good grade on it like an A but I doubt it because I don't pay enough attention in class and I know it too. Well good night.

Love,
Tony

FRIDAY, 6 APRIL 1979

Dear Ty,

I went to Jack's today and he almost got caught today. She came in about 45 minutes early and that was so fucked. I walked right out the front door with the new *Blueboy* and *Honcho*. "Oh Well." Then I went to the book stand and they wanted to see an ID but I don't have an ID. "Oh Well." Then I wanted to go to the mall but did not have the time so fuck that idea, then I started to thumb and got picked up by this guy who looked at every girl (fat or skinny) on the streets so fuck that too. Then he dropped me off by the bus stop and I walked back to McDonald's and these two guys were laying in the grass in front of the library and one had on shorts and no joke he had the biggest balls and I looked right at them and he laughted (ha ha) and there were these two guys in McDonald's, body builders, and one had the nicest pouch through his jeans and was a total babe too. Well that's all, oh tomorrow <u>Tyler</u>. Good night.

Love,
Tony

SATURDAY, 7 APRIL 1979

Dear Ty,

Well I went to bowling today and in the tearoom, me and Tyler sat peeping through the glory hole in the wall at each other. Then he asked if I could make myself cum and I said YES like a dumbass and he said "cum" then and I started to beat my meat and could not cum then he walked out I was so pissed. Well I don't think me and Tyler will ever have a love affair. Too bad. Tonight we are going to go to Dad's and are looking for houses in the morning. I have the worst stomachache in the world so I cannot go out like last time, what a dud. I hope me and Tyler get together somehow but I doubt it. Well, that's life. He is a little stuck-up anyway. He thinks he is better than everyone else. Oh his friend has the nicest cock in the world it is so big. Boy would I love that. And he was showing it off to everyone at the bowling alley. "Oh Well." Good night.

Love,

Tony

SUNDAY, 8 APRIL 1979

Dear Ty,

Well we went house hunting today and looked at so many houses that they all looked alike. Dad's next door neighbor has a short arm but he plays ping-pong OK and the guy he lives with has a nice bod, real skinny but nice. They went swimming today in the pool and that water was ice cold, they are crazy. He had on this little diving bathing suit but you could not really tell how big he was but I think he was about six inches or seven inches long, not bad. The guy with a half arm was not big at all, about four or five inches long. Not big at all to my standards. Well that's all the cocks I got to see (through clothes). Well good night.

Love,

Tony

MONDAY, 9 APRIL 1979

Dear Ty,

Today I went to the bowling alley to see if I could get some cock. And there was this guy who kept looking at my cock but did not make any moves or show me his cock, it was weird. Once I saw him go in the bowling alley to go to the tearoom and leave. I don't know what his act was. "Oh Well." I saw some pretty nice cocks in the tearoom but not much, it was a slow day totally. Then I went to McDonald's for lunch and the guy who works there had boxers on and tight pants, or no underwear—he had a nice cock, no doubt about it. And I sat across from this guy who had a nice cock too, he was rubbing himself right there in the place. Then I got hard and he did not even notice me at all. Total dud. Tomorrow the probation officer comes at 8:00 in the morning. I don't know what for but I will tell tomorrow. I might go to the bowling alley tomorrow I hope. Good night.

Love,
Tony

TUESDAY, 10 APRIL 1979

Dear Ty,

Well the probation dud came and I have to go to counseling again. How FUCKED. I did not have time to go to the bowling alley but did go out at midnight tonight and I went to the Plankhouse to pick up a trick but no luck. But I did meet this guy who was so drunk it was pitiful. And he barfed in the back of his truck, how sickening huh. And he was staring right at my cock and it was bulging right out of my pants and he said he wished he was "a little straighter" right after he was looking at my cock. I asked what he meant and he said that he was not so drunk. Too bad huh. I went to my new flame's house and looked in his window and he was fast asleep. He is so weird though. But he has a nice bod TOTALLY. I have to call him, he lives on my route, and I have to call Mark (the fox). Well that's all for tonight. Good night.

Love,

Tony

WEDNESDAY, 11 APRIL 1979

Dear Ty,

Well Mom caught me last night and I told her that I was jogging and she said "SURE" like always and now I think I am grounded again, what a dud. She will not tell me how long I am grounded for like always so I did not ask yet. We went to Gemco today and they have the skates I want in size ten. They won't last long but who cares. I am going to rip them off anyway like everything else I have. I did not rip off this diary!!! Surprise. Surprise. I got my thing back from Barbizon today and am going to get an interview as soon as I get my hair done. It looks so bad all the time I hate it so much. Well that's all for tonight. I did not call my new love or Mark today. Tomorrow I hope. Good night.

Love,

Tony

THURSDAY, 12 APRIL 1979

Dear Ty,

Well I called my new love and Mark and they were not home. I have to think of what to say to both of them before I call back.

Dad called and said, "Don't ever go out at that time of night," etc. We were going to go to the show but Eric did not want to like always. So we (me and Mom) are going to go see SUPERMAN tomorrow. What a babe, he is foxy—get off. I am having thoughts about taking money from Jim again because I am broke but if I got caught I would be arrested for blackmail. That's all I need right now. I would take about $500.00 or so but that is not much I don't think (yes it is) but he won't think so. It will take a while to figure it all out. Well Good night.

Love,
Tony

FRIDAY, 13 APRIL 1979

Dear Ty,

Today is Friday the 13th and Good Friday, a day of bad and good luck so everything will work out I hope. Well I put Neet on my balls and asshole and around so I can be hairless. I cut the liner out of my bathing suit and now you can see every bump and bulge in my shorts. Now it's off to the swap meet to get a trick to get it on with I hope. Tomorrow I am going to go to Gemco and get some skates and put them out on the patio and get them Sunday morning when I do my papers. I babysat Jay and made five dollars tonight and saw Andy Stevens (the Bastard) in THE FURY. It was so bitchen, he only had on a bathing suit, what a babe. Well Good night.

Love,
Tony

SATURDAY, 14 APRIL 1979

Dear Ty,

Well I did not have time to go to bowling today and see Tyler. It was no tap anyway. I got up at noon and Dad came over at 2:00 so I had no time to do anything. We went to Grandma's sister's birthday today in LA and we went to get a card at Thrifty and the new *Playgirl* is out with Jon Voight on the cover. I hope it is a good one with a lot of cocks in it. I will go to our Thrifty tomorrow and find out, I cannot wait to find out what the centerfold looks like. Well I have to go to bed now to get up and do my papers in the morning. Good night.

Love,
Tony

SUNDAY, 15 APRIL 1979

Dear Ty,

Happy Easter. I got up at 6:00 a.m. to do my papers and Eric was not up yet and they were so big. Well I did not do anything with Mom or Dad or Eric. I went to Sav-on to turn in my film and then I went to Alpha Beta and I got a hard-on and this guy who works there noticed it thank god, and then the store manager thought I put something in my pants and I was about to say that it was all me and all real and I would prove it to her right there but I did not. I saw the new *Playgirl* and the centerfold has the bod, face, and the COCK for a centerfold. I am going to go get it tomorrow I hope I can but with my luck…I am going to call my new love and Mark tomorrow. He was with Jim today and they looked so delicious out there in their shorts. Good night.

Love,
Tony

MONDAY, 16 APRIL 1979

Dear Ty,

Well I got caught ditching again, what a dud huh. Now I am grounded again no doubt. I stayed after school today and watched drill team, they are so bad—half of them don't even know the routine. I might join the $1.98 beauty contest Wednesday the 18th but I don't know if Mom called Dad yet but she probably did no doubt. She tells him everything that happens. I wonder when we get to see more houses. I want to move and be close to Jack. Well Good night.

Love,
Tony

TUESDAY, 17 APRIL 1979

Dear Ty,

Well I am going to enter the $1.98 beauty contest tomorrow I hope if I don't chicken out. I went to Thrifty and got the May *Playgirl* and what a bunch of babes. They have this section on <u>tight pants</u> and some of the cocks are huge through the jeans and they are all nice. I got ten goldfish today and don't have any fish food for them so they have to wait. I saw this guy at Sound Factory who had the nicest cock through his jeans. I wonder if the guy at Sound Factory is gay or not, either one of them. He's cute though. I am going to make up a dance to "Le Freak" (as I go). I hope I don't blow it. Well Good night.

Love,
Tony

Dear Ty,

I chickened out and did not try out after all. Now I wish I would have but I will try out when they have the next tryouts. I want to be in the contest so bad though but I will feel like an ass totally. But who cares? I don't know how long I am grounded for I will ask. Tomorrow I am going to take a disco song and we will figure out a dance routine for me to do in the show. I don't have the faintest idea what to dance to but who knows. I will figure out something to do. Well Good night.

Love,
Tony

P.S. The Village People are having a concert this summer and I want to go and have not called new love or Mark yet, tomorrow.

THURSDAY, 19 APRIL 1979

Dear Ty,

Well I forgot to call Mark or new love and I forgot to call about the Village People, oh well. I took the records today and Mr. Brooks would not let me and Lupe get a record player from the library. I don't know why. So he says he will bring his little girl's tomorrow but she won't let him I know. I cannot believe how popular I am getting. I know anybody who is anybody who is anyone. It is so bitchen knowing everyone at school. I think I can get the guy who live on the corner of Sequoia and Medina. Lori has that house on her route and that guy is gay for sure. Well Good night.

Love,
Tony

FRIDAY, 20 APRIL 1979

Dear Ty,

Well I got his number from Lori and his name is Don and his number is 527-8943. I keep calling but he is not home. I will call tomorrow and ask if he wants to get it on, then when he sees me he will just die. I hope. Mom went out with Jim and I went to McDonald's for dinner and to Gemco, the bowling alley, and Simi Liquors. Gemco was a dud and three quarters and at the bowling alley I saw two tiny little cocks and Simi Liquors has *Honcho* again and I am going to try so hard to get one because I can't ditch school or else it is off to jail that's what the probation officer said. Well the tickets for Village People did not go on sale yet so I have to wait. Good night.

Love,
Tony

SATURDAY, 21 APRIL 1979

Dear Ty,

Well today is my lucky day. I went to bowling and into the can, and Tyler was sitting on the throne like always. I came so close to cumming and someone walked in on us I was so pissed. We were looking through the hole in the wall like always and he was beating off so I could see him. I just about had a heart attack right there in the tearoom and he would not cum and he bent down and I started sucking on him and it was so fun. Then he started to give me a hand job, then got up and started to go out and he said "cum" and I said "why?" and then someone came in and he walked out. "Oh Well." Then I went in later after another guy who works there and he would not let me see his cock, he was ready to leave and he was hard, about six inches long, and then left like a bolt of lightening. Oh, I

called Don and he has not been home all day long. I got a partici-
pation trophy in bowling. It is so little. Well Good night.

Love,

Tony

SUNDAY, 22 APRIL 1979

Dear Ty,

Well I called Don today and he answered the phone. At first he
did not remember me. Then he did and said he has "lived here all his
life" and to "keep my secret under your hat." "Oh Well." I want to get
it on with him so bad. Well I never thought I would live to see the day
that we put our house up for sale but we really did it though. Mom,
Jackie, and Jay are going to live together in Camarillo maybe. And Pete
is going to move to Las Vegas maybe. He does not like the weather
here, he wants a drier climate to live in. Well I babysat Jay tonight
I don't know for how long. Well that's all for tonight. Good night.

Love,

Tony

MONDAY, 23 APRIL 1979

Dear Ty,

Well they put up the for-sale sign in the front yard I cannot believe
my eyes when I look at it in front of our house. Every other house in
the cul-de-sac has been sold a couple of times but this is a first in the
history of the Robertsons I am so glad. I wonder what Bob thought.
Who cares what he thought anyway. I hate his guts. Anyway one of
my fish died last night. "Oh Well." Well that's all for tonight.

Love,

Tony

TUESDAY, 24 APRIL 1979

Dear Ty,

Well they put another sign on the for-sale sign that says "swim pool" instead of "swimming pool" how dumb. Lori might quit her route and I would take it so fast. If she does quit and I do her route and mine, I would make over $100.00 a month. How bitchen that would be if I made that much a month but with my luck she will keep her route. Then I will only make my measly $50.00 a month. When we move I want to get a route with the *Herald Examiner* then I will make some money and if I sell me, I will make more money so I have to be a good big boy until we move. OK well Good night.

Love,
Tony

WEDNESDAY, 25 APRIL 1979

Dear Ty,

Well Lori is going to keep her route, see I knew she would because I have the worst luck in the world. After school we sold popcorn to raise money to go to Knott's Berry Farm with the Annual class. Well I have to go see what probation is tomorrow, what a dud I know that for sure. I won't get busted very bad I know that for sure. I took my camera to school today like always and we wasted a lot of film like always. I have to figure out how I am going to call Mark "the babe." Well Good night.

Love,
Tony

THURSDAY, 26 APRIL 1979

Dear Ty,

Well I figured out a way to talk to Mark and it worked. He was home alone and I went collecting and we started talking and his fly was open. I think he did it on purpose. I hope so. And I called him, panicked, and hung up like a dummy. I can talk to him face to face better than on the phone. Well it's raining right now so no PE tomorrow I hope. I think I will just go up to him and ask why he was reading *Cosmopolitan* and why he had toilet paper wrapped around his cock and if he is gay. If he asks how I know I will tell him when I went into their house last summer and the light was on so I was curious and looked in the window to see what he was doing and whose room it was I was looking into—and it was him. So I want to tell him that I would have done it for him if he likes. Good night.

Love,
Tony

FRIDAY, 27 APRIL 1979

Dear Ty,

I got to go to the dance so I guess I am not grounded anymore but I am not going to go anywhere without asking first. We are going to LA tomorrow and tomorrow is the open house so we have to get everything ready. At the dance, Lori wanted me to ask Andra to dance but I chickened out. She is the cutest girl at school and has a bitchen bod so I guess I am not gay I am a bisexua.l So what, so I want to go to bed with a man or a women, who cares—no biggie is it? No. Well I was going to go over the hill to work at the spastic kid's place with Lori but Mom said no and before she said yes.

What a FUCKEN BITCH she is. I am trying to stop cussing. I have a feeling something is going to happen tomorrow or Sunday. Good night.

Love,
Tony

SATURDAY, 28 APRIL 1979

Dear Ty,

Well we are at Grandma's house and I am watching *Saturday Night Live* right now. Today we dropped Mom off at the airport and she went to San Jose and stayed at Jim's apartment over the weekend. I did not ask where he was but who cares anyway. Well nothing happened today so something will happen tomorrow I just know it. Well I got to see Aunt Liz's baby cousin Marvin Jr., and Marlie my cousin likes her little baby brother. She wanted a brother anyway and she got one. The baby does not cry much but when he does he gives it all he's got. He just screams on and on as loud as can be. Well that's all for now. Good night.

Love,
Tony

SUNDAY, 29 APRIL 1979

Dear Ty,

You will never guess what happened today. Something happened to Bobbie my aunt. She was out cold and had a seizure (I think). Now it is 12:00 a.m. midnight and I have school tomorrow. What am I going to say to everyone? They will call me skinhead I know it. Especially Lupe because I always cut her down so low it is pathetic. We went to the hospital it is so far from Grandma's house I can't believe it. Well we were there so long I could not believe it and did not eat until 9:00 p.m. We saw Bobbie, she looks so bad but she ain't going to die. I know that. Well that's all. Good night.

Love,

Tony

MONDAY, 30 APRIL 1979

Dear Ty,

Well guess what, I got a new pen finally. It is a lot better than my old one. Well I got all the smart remarks from everyone especially LUPE, a skinhead and the oldest one of them all buzzzzzzzzz. I got my pictures back that I took of my hamster and Arnold and Missy it is about time anyway. I went to Alpha Beta for the first time since the shorts incident. "Oh Well." My new pen is called a Spree it works pretty good huh. Tomorrow we might go to the show and see *Superman* I hope it's good and not just a fake like people say. Well Good night.

Love,

Tony

TUESDAY, 1 MAY 1979

Dear Ty,

Well we went to see *Superman* finally and me and Mom sat in the front and Eric and Mark sat in the back. Well during intermission I went to the can like always and I think this guy who was in there was gay because he just stood there and then flushed and left "Oh Well." Then I went back in and he was blocking the door. When I went to go in he smiled and left and this other guy was standing there going to piss and I look over and he had the hugest cock I have seen down there I could not believe it and he looked like he was a little hard but I don't know maybe you never know do you! Well tomorrow is the big ninth-grade picture during sixth offering. I want to go to the swap meet on Sunday. Good night.

Love,
Tony

WEDNESDAY, 2 MAY 1979

Dear Ty,

Well we took the big picture today and I was one person away from Dan when they took the picture before Wes, this fat kid, came and sat down between us. I was so pissed I was ready to say "move please I want to be next to Dan please" but I did not. Then everyone was wearing Sunkist skirts and they made a great big pyramid and I of course was taking pictures. Don't I always carry that thing around everywhere I go. I might make about $60.00 this month, how bitchen, and my bill was only $103.64 that ain't much at all. I am not arguing. This morning I was late and Lupe said we had to walk to school from Gemco because her mother ran out of gas and now we have to bring a note from our mothers. Good night.

Love,
Tony

THURSDAY, 3 MAY 1979

Dear Ty,

Well Mom wrote me a note and she wrote "late to homeroom" and all I did was erase "homeroom" so it says I was late, no time on it. Well I got *Bad Girls* from Sound Factory and Mom got it and got the cassette instead of the 8-track so I have to take it back tomorrow. Our homeroom played volleyball this morning and we lost. I knew we would. I am going to take the cassette at lunchtime tomorrow and go to McDonald's for lunch I hope. We have a quiz tomorrow in Oceanography on dissecting and we dissect on Monday or Tuesday. I hope Monday. I have to pass if I want to dissect anything. I will I know it. Well Good night.

Love,
Tony

FRIDAY, 4 MAY 1979

Dear Ty,

Well we had the quiz in Oceanography and it was so easy I could not believe it. I went to McDonald's for lunch and to Sound Factory and got the tape. It is good, especially the song "Bad Girls." Well the pictures I took of the pyramid came out so good I could not believe it. Now Brooks says we have to charge our friends for the pictures because the paper cost 25 cents for 8 x 10s so we have to charge for them. "Oh Well." Well Marco can go to the Donna Summer concert with me. I will send for the tickets as soon as possible. Well Good night.

Love,
Tony

SATURDAY, 5 MAY 1979

Dear Ty,

Well I went down to the bowling alley and into the tearoom and there was an out-of-order sign on one of the stalls and I went into the other one and the piece of metal was gone from the glory hole and I took the out-of-order sign off the door and sat down. Then Tyler and me were sitting there and he got pissed because I would not cum or do anything and went storming out like a bolt of lighting. This other guy was sitting on the can and he was beating and then stuck it right through the hole and I made him cum—and his son goes to my school? I stayed up all night and this afternoon. After bowling I went to Gemco and put skates outside and now have to go get them early in the morning very early. I hope I can. Staying up all night was so much fun, first and last time I think. Well Good night.

Love,
Tony

SUNDAY, 6 MAY 1979

Dear Ty,

Well I went down to Gemco at about 5:30 a.m. and there were about 20 to 25 cars in line for gas and by the time I got down there it was too sunny out so I could not get them I was so pissed!!!! We had open house today and one family showed up I could not believe it. It is because it was listed in Camarillo and not Simi so we could have listed with Kim's mom after all but we listed with Pete's friend Ben something. I wonder if we dissect tomorrow, I hope so. I can't wait. Well Good night.

Love,
Tony

MONDAY, 7 MAY 1979

Dear Ty,

Well I meant to take my camera to school today but I forgot to I am so dumb. We would have just wasted film anyway. So no biggie. Well we listed our house with Ben Santeze and I don't think Pete works in real estate anymore I don't know why but who knows what is happening. Dad came over and he called and I told him to stop at Northridge Cameras and get me an autowinder and I got it, how bitchen. Tomorrow I will take it to school and try it out with film in it. It will be so great at least it works and ain't like Pete's (ha ha). Well that's all for tonight. Well Good night.

Love,
Tony

TUESDAY, 8 MAY 1979

Dear Ty,

Guess what happened last night, I had a wet dream and when I woke up there was cum in the bed and all over my cock and now I guess I can beat off till I cum. I hope so I could not try tonight but as soon as I can I will. It rained for about 30 minutes today, it was pouring too I could not believe it…and then it was as sunny as can be. I took my camera to school today and I only used two rolls of film and there is a picture of me jumping off the outside stage and I am in midair it is so bitchen I could not believe it. On June 2nd the ninth grade goes to Magic Mountain and I think we will have to get partners and I am going to try to be Dan's partner. I hope I can and he does not go with someone else I know he will. Good Night.

Love,
Tony

WEDNESDAY, 9 MAY 1979

Dear Ty,

Well Bobbie had another seizure today and is in intensive care. This might be the big one I hope not even though I don't think she is my favorite aunt. I don't want her to die she still has a while yet I hope? They still have not said anything about the Magic Mountain trip and we are to go to Knott's Berry Farm on June 9th the day after the 9th grade formal, we will be so tired to death. Well I will just come home and go to bed and then in the morning shower and go to the school and now I have to save my money for the trip. I have to ask someone to the dance but I don't know. Well Good Night.

Love,
Tony

THURSDAY, 10 MAY 1979

Dear Ty,

Today they put the 9th grade picture in the office and I am standing on my knees and higher than everyone else. Dan looks good like always. What if one day like ten years from now me and Dan are lying in a bed arm in arm reading this. He will just laugh and so will I. I hope it comes true someday. I pray. He has such a BITCHEN BOD and is a cutie I can't believe it. I went to the Plankhouse and Denny's to see some cock and did not see any, what a dud. I saw some big ones through the jeans but that's all. We played volleyball this morning and lost and no one came because they thought we had a bye and tomorrow we play again and we better win so I have to get up at 7:00 a.m. and take a shower and wash my hair. Good Night.

Love,
Tony

FRIDAY, 11 MAY 1979

Dear Ty,

Well we played volleyball this morning and we lost the first game because we were late again and the second game was hot. The score was 10–12. It was 0–8 and we caught up and then we lost the ball and they won it figures like always huh. I don't know if I can have a graduation party and I hope she says yes. But bitch will say no. We are going to go to the Plankhouse for Mother's Day for champagne brunch I hope. I went looking for Dan's house and could not find it. I have to get his phone number and get the guts to ask him to go swimming but I don't know if I have the guts. I don't know what I will do tomorrow, there are these bugs in my room and they are everywhere I turn and I sprayed them and have to see tomorrow. Good Night.

Love,
Tony

SATURDAY, 12 MAY 1979

Dear Ty,

Well I went to the bowling alley and just riding around at the bowling alley. The glory hole is still there and hot as ever. I want to put one in the can at Gemco because it is hot too. First, me and Tyler were sitting there and he put toilet paper in the hole and I did not make a move and he got up and walked out. No biggie. Then this other guy was beating his meat and he had the biggest knob I have ever seen in my life and he shot his load and left. He was married anyway. I saw these three guys walking to the bowling alley and they were shirtless and had the bitchenest bods but did not go into the can. I went to Coast Valley Spa & Racquetball and the guy who works there had on shorts and he has the bitchenest bod I wonder if he is gay. Who knows. I went to Gemco and the skates are still out there so I am going to get them at about 3 or 4 in the morning. Good Night.

Love,
Tony

SUNDAY, 13 MAY 1979

Dear Ty,

Well I got my skates this morning at about 3:00 a.m. and they work so bitchen. I did my route on them and it is not so easy. I don't know when I will tell Mom how I got them. I will tell her I bought them from a garage sale or something. Well Dad came over and we were going to go to the Plankhouse for Mother's Day brunch but it was 1 ½ hours to wait to eat so fuck it. All we did was clean house. Mom said I can't have a party so no party I think. I don't give up easy, so just wait. We are going to see the house this week, soon I hope. Well Good Night.

Love,
Tony

MONDAY, 14 MAY 1979

Dear Ty,

Well today kicked off Sadie Hawkins week and today was Crazy Socks Day and tomorrow is Shorts Day, how bitchen huh. I am going to wear shorts no doubt. Tomorrow is Oceanography and we are going to dissect a crayfish it looks so sick. Me and Lori got in a fight with Kim over the 9th grade picture and now she is mad at us and we tried to make up but she is such a bitch. She gets mad like her mom and dad that's why she gets so pissed all the time. Well that's all for tonight. Good Night.

Love,
Tony

TUESDAY, 15 MAY 1979

Dear Ty,

Well it was so cold this morning that I did not put my shorts on until it got hotter. It was so cold, not that many people wore shorts so it was still no biggie; yes it was because I like to wear shorts in the open. Ha ha. Dale wore shorts and boxers and you could see the outline of his cock. I still want to see Victor's so bad I don't have much time before school is out. Dan went on a field trip to CBS studios in LA so I did not see him in shorts. "Oh Well." I go to counseling tomorrow about the tearoom. We dissected today and it was no biggie I don't think but I did not tell him that of course not; I don't want to fail that class. Mom found out about the skates because she found them. I will tell you the whole story tomorrow. Good Night.

Love,
Tony

WEDNESDAY, 16 MAY 1979

Dear Ty,

Today was Crazy Hat day and I did not wear a hat but Lori brought this weird-looking thing that looks like this. I don't have the slightest idea of what it was but I wore it all day but last period. "Oh Well." We were going to sell snow cones today but it is tomorrow. I went to my shrink and he's pretty cool. He just asked about me, what happened, and that kind of stuff. I want him to hypnotize me to skate better, do my schoolwork, not lie, not cuss, bowl and golf better, and not be shy around people I don't know. I hope he does it next time I go down there I hope so. Well Good Night.

Love,

Tony

THURSDAY, 17 MAY 1979

Dear Ty,

Well everything happened today. We went and saw the new house it is so bitchen. I think it is pretty big inside. It looks small from the outside but it has the gnarliest kitchen sink...I am going to do the cooking from now on. We went to see Birmingham High School and it don't look so hot from the outside and there is this long skate and bike trail in the big park. There are enough things to do over there all day, how bitchen. My hamster got out last night and Missy got it and killed it. It had a long, long life compared to some of my other hamsters. The bugs are coming from the hamster's food. They are little black bugs, I sprayed them and they are all dead I hope. We sold snow comes and I think we did OK for the first time. The next time we will do better I hope???? I don't know who I am going to ask to formal. Maybe Kristi, Tiffany, or Jeanette. I had an affair with her once so you never know. Well Good Night.

Love,

Tony

FRIDAY, 18 MAY 1979

Dear Ty,

Well I went to the dance tonight and it was so much fun. We sold pictures and went through three rolls of film and we sold popcorn and it was so much fun. We made about $72.00. That ain't bad is it. Mom went to see Bobbie and Dad came and spent the night. Tomorrow is Kristy's surprise birthday party I hope there are people I know there. I know Tracy will be there but I don't know about Lori and Kristi. They won't I know it that's like them. I want to ask Wendy to go to the formal with me. If she says no I will die and then I will ask Tiffany and she won't say no I don't think. Well Good Night.

Love,
Tony

SATURDAY, 19 MAY 1979

Dear Ty,

Well I went to Kristie's party and I did not know that many people but it was OK. I got her: *He's the Greatest Dancer* and *We Are Family* by Sister Sledge and *Star Love* by Cheryl Lynn and I took it home and acted like I could not find it in my records and now I can listen to it a while and give it back to her. That's mean but who cares she gets it back anyways. Mom has asked about the skates but I have not gotten in trouble yet thank god. I hope I don't get in trouble that's all I need right now. The bugs are back now they are under the bed so I'll clean under the bed tomorrow. I want to go to the swap meet tomorrow and get a trick. After graduation I want to go out to Charlie Brown's, Hungry Tiger, Benihana's, or someplace like that. I did not ask Wendy yet. Tomorrow. Good Night.

Love,
Tony

SUNDAY, 20 MAY 1979

David's Birthday

Dear Ty,

I forgot all about David's birthday. I will get a card tomorrow I hope. I did not do anything special today but sleep. I fell asleep on the couch for four or five hours today and I did not have enough time to go to the swap meet today…it was gloomy out anyway. I want to go on *The Gong Show* and sing "Star Love" by Cheryl Lynn and win the $500.00. I could use the money badly. I want to go on there so bad it is pitiful. Mom has not said a word about the skates yet so I hope she does not say anything. The new *Playgirl* came out and I did not get a chance to look at it yet. I will don't worry. I have to get the $15 and call Jack tomorrow. I think we sell snow cones tomorrow. Don't know. Good Night.

Love,

Tony

MONDAY, 21 MAY 1979

Dear Ty,

Well I got a new pen as you can tell. I ripped it off from Ralph's easy stuff. We have to pick a candidate from the Annual to be in the princess ceremonies and I am the guy who got picked from Annual. I hope so I want to do it so bad but I know I won't get to for some reason. We sold snow cones today and made about $30, not bad for a cold day huh. I could not call Jack or get David a card I forgot my money for Magic Mountain so I will pay tomorrow for sure. I am going to take better care of me…the face and the bod and the ass as nice as I can? I hope. Good Night.

Love,

Tony

TUESDAY, 22 MAY 1979

Dear Ty,

I still don't know who got picked for the princess ceremonies yet. I called Jack and he fell off a ladder and might not be back to work at all. I hope he is alright. I want to go over there soon as I can, which might not be very soon. I got David a card but forgot to send it, so tomorrow. I asked Mary Kay if she thinks Wendy would go to the formal with me and she did not know. I am so nervous about asking her. Tomorrow I go to counseling and I will ask if he will hypnotize me so I will get a good grade on Billing's test on Thursday. I better get a good grade. I am going to study so hard, hard, hard. Well Good Night.

Love,
Tony

WEDNESDAY, 23 MAY 1979

Dear Ty,

Well I went to counseling this evening and all we did was talk and talk. Mom called about the skates and talked to him about them and he brought it up and said, "Do you think they are hot?" I said no and that was that about the skates. Today in the *PennySaver* there was an ad about waterbeds that you do by yourself for $69.95 and that is cheap. It comes with a mattress, liner, and frame or heater. I am going to buy the heater by itself, and get the frame, and I am going to get a double bed. It is 4 ½ feet by 7 feet, not bad for $70 huh? He did not hypnotize me tonight I could not say anything about it. Well tomorrow is Billing's test. I am studying my butt off so I can get a good grade. Well Good Night.

Love,
Tony

THURSDAY, 24 MAY 1979

Dear Ty,

Well you will never guess what happened, I am not Jill's escort in the princess ceremonies. I was so pissed she asked Joe, the guy who she likes. I was so MAD but I did not say anything, I should have. I am so dumb. Well we took the test in Billing's and he read all the Scantron cards back to us and did not call my name. I was so nervous and I went up to him and asked and I got 47 out of 50 I could not believe it. It was so easy I hope finals are this easy I pray. There were 60 possible and he did not correct the written part, I got a ten, I know; so I only got three wrong out of the whole thing, not bad at all. Well Good Night.

Love,
Tony

FRIDAY, 25 MAY 1979

Dear Ty,

Well I got 54 on the test I thought I would do a lot better than that. My grade is a 73% or a C-. Today I walked home with Dan. I was so nervous but I calmed down a little. He showed me where he lives and I told him about were I live and that we have a pool and I said, "You can come swimming someday." I hope tomorrow or this weekend. I want to go to the beach so bad this weekend since it is a three-day weekend. I wonder if Dan is going to go to Magic Mountain. I hope so, I pray so. I went swimming tonight it was so cold but the heater works finally. That is why Dan, Lori, and Kristi can come swimming tomorrow or over the weekend. I hope I have all my work done so they can come. Good Night.

Love,
Tony

SATURDAY, 26 MAY 1979

Dear Ty,

Well I did not do anything exciting today but I went swimming with Lori and I have to go collect so I will have money for Magic Mountain. I went to Dan's but he was not home so I went down to Wagon Trails and then to Sandy's Pool Supply, then back to Dan's. Tuesday I have to ask how many sisters he has. When they come to the door they are all cuties just like Dan. Then he went collecting because he was going out to dinner that night. I found him down the street and he could not go swimming because he was going to dinner and spending the night at Dan's. We might go to the beach tomorrow, I want to go on Monday. I hope it rains or something. Good Night.

Love,
Tony

SUNDAY, 27 MAY 1979

Dear Ty,

Well my papers were late this morning because it RAINED. So I don't think we will go to the beach today, I hope tomorrow. We cleaned out the garage and what a mess. We rented a trailer and took all the junk to the dump and we went to KMart to see if they had boogie boards because Eric said they had them for $4.99. That ain't bad at all. I did not go to Dan's but I got his phone number from Sydelle who used to like him. I don't blame her at all. His phone number is 522-9236. Now I have to get up the guts to call and ask if he wants to go to the beach tomorrow, if we go at all. Well Good Night.

Love,
Tony

MONDAY, 28 MAY 1979

No school—Memorial Day

Dear Ty,

Well I had a morning paper and I sort of wish they all were morning papers. We had to clean under the work bench and then Dad got mad at me and Eric and he said something to Eric and I asked what he said and Eric said, "We are not going to the beach." So I got mad at Dad and he yelled at me for skating in the house and said take them off so I got even madder at him. Then I fell asleep on the couch for three or four hours and I made a cake and it looked so pitiful. And I did not get the guts to call Dan so today was a total DUD and a half. Well Good Night.

Love,

Tony

TUESDAY, 29 MAY 1979

Dear Ty,

Well I did not see Dan all day long. And he was there I know it for sure but I did not see him and that is unusual, very unusual. I don't know where he was but what can I say. Tomorrow I go to my physiologist and I hope he hypnotizes me. I pray. My luck, he won't. Tomorrow I might take my skates to school and skate I hope. They will probably get taken away. Four more days until Magic Mountain. I was going to ask Dad if he is going but I did not see him so I could not ask. "Oh Well." I will ask tomorrow I hope. If he is not going I will just die. Well Good Night.

Love,

Tony

WEDNESDAY, 30 MAY 1979

Arnold's Birthday

Dear Ty,

I forgot all about Arnold's birthday today. He does not need anything anyway the little pig. Well Dan is not going to Magic Mountain because he says he does not have the money but he has a paper route so he should. He said he has to get a tux and stuff for the formal but he should still have money I have to talk to him. I hoped someone does not have to go so he can go. I went to my shrink this evening and we talked like always. He taught me this relaxing exercise to do so when I get hypnotized it will work better on me I hope? Well three more days until Magic Mountain. And <u>Dan</u> IS <u>going</u>. Good Night.

Love,

Tony

THURSDAY, 31 MAY 1979

Dear Ty,

Well I got my pants for Magic Mountain finally. I got painter pants instead of baggies they were all so ugly, it was pathetic. I wrote Dan a note during English and I said, "Write back," so I will probably get a note tomorrow morning. This guy Berry paid to go to Magic Mountain and now he cannot go so maybe if I talk Dan into going he will go. I hope so. I would not go to bed with him because I don't know I have too much respect for him I guess I don't know. We talk more now. I hope he writes me a note tonight or tomorrow so he can go to Magic Mountain. Brooks bought a light bulb for the enlarger so time to take some porn pictures of me. Good Night.

P.S. Two days till Magic Mountain.

Love,

Tony

FRIDAY, 1 JUNE 1979

Dear Ty,

Well Dan is not going to go to Magic Mountain because Barry can go and if he misses baseball practice he cannot play in the double-header on Sunday. So I guess I will live. I am going to hang around with Lori and Kim probably. I saw Dale's cock in PE today and it is so nice I would love to have it down my mouth and I saw Dan's too. It is nice and fat and big it is bigger than mine hard, for sure. I still would not go to bed with him. I am not lying I swear to <u>God</u> on the Holy Bible. Dan's phone number is not 522-9236, it is 522-2851. Sydelle is wrong because he told me the right number. Tomorrow is Magic Mountain, how bitchen. I will tell you all about it. Good Night.

Love,
Tony

SATURDAY, 2 JUNE 1979

Dear Ty,

Well we went to Magic Mountain and it was so much fun. Colossus was closed, what a dud, so we went on everything else that was open except the Mountain Express and I wanted to go on that because it is so radical. At the games I spent $10.00 trying to win a great big Woodstock and Jeff spent $1.00 and won I was so pissed at him and we went to Spillikin Corners and made these candles that you dip in different colored wax and make them layered. Then we went to this place called Memories on Tin and we put on old-fashioned clothes and got our picture taken and it was so fun if you could see it you would die laughing. I saw some nice cocks today even though I was with all my friends. On the Jet Stream we got soaked to death but we had a good time all day long. I bought a great big sucker for $2.99 and that is not bad at all. I still wish Dan could have gone he would have had so much fun totally. I took my camera and took a lot of pictures. Good Night.

Love,
Tony

SUNDAY, 3 JUNE 1979

Dear Ty,

I went over to Dan's house at about 11:30 and he was already gone to the game and it was an away game at a school a long ways away. The game was not until 1:00 so it had to be a long ways away. My papers were an hour late this morning but who cares. Dan was going to call but didn't, they lost so he was probably depressed so he did not want to call. I think Mark is a closet gay to the max. I was going to go out and look in the window and see if he is gay. He moved a piece of cardboard away from the window by his bed. He wants me to look in the window, if I'm right. I hope so. Well Good Night.

Love,
Tony

MONDAY, 4 JUNE 1979

Dear Ty,

Well Brooks had a party tonight for the Annual class and I had so much fun. First we rode his horse named Tony and he has another one named Jill. The pony looks like Jill. We went swimming and sat in the Jacuzzi and it was about 100 degrees to 103 degrees hot. But it was so nice just sitting in the hot water. Sunday on the tenth we are going to go to Knott's Berry Farm and we got an extra ticket and David is going to go too. That will be so great, I will want to leave and go to his house! So I can see it for the first time. I did not talk to Dan that much but I will start hanging around him more and talk to him more. Well Good Night.

Love,
Tony

TUESDAY, 5 JUNE 1979

Dear Ty,

Well I had to go to probation for the first time and Alan got called out to an emergency so I don't have to go until the first Tuesday of next month. I have to start beating my meat so I can make myself cum. I saw Mark today and I was going to ask him if I could suck his cock but I have to get up the nerve. I might go to the mall but I will be so careful this time. I hope it is someone else and not who I got busted with before or else fuck it. No possible way I will try anything. I don't need to get busted again. Well I go tomorrow to my shrink. Tell you all about it. Good Night.

Love,
Tony

WEDNESDAY, 6 JUNE 1979

Dear Ty,

I went to my shrink and he talked to me for about 15 to 20 minutes and then to Mom and Dad. We are going to a picnic on Saturday with Dad and they have a pool so I might get a trick there I hope so. Today we got to wear shorts to school just the 9th graders only, because of Picnic Day. It was like almost anything goes and we had a bunch of events and the winner gets a 15-foot banana split for their homeroom and the annual homeroom (my homeroom) gets one too so I don't care that we did not get to play. Anyway who cares. Friday is Billing's final test for Oceanography so I have to go to that class at least, then to the mall I hope. After the formal I am going to go look in Mark's window and let him catch me maybe. No, I could get in a lot of trouble if he is not gay. But I hope he is gay anyway. Good Night.

Love,

Tony

THURSDAY, 7 JUNE 1979

Dear Ty,

Well tomorrow is the formal. I got shoes, a shirt, and the stuff I need. I asked Kristi to the dance but she thought I was joking (ha ha). She will go with me and she knows it. I do not see Dan that much lately, I have to talk to him more so we are good, good friends when we move. Then I will write and he will write back I hope. I have less than 24 hours before the final test in Oceanography. I hope it is easy, I have studied so much that my brain is about to crack open. I hope the annuals come by homeroom tomorrow so we can sign them. I want everyone to sign it that is popular. The rest will just be friends. Good Night.

Love,

Tony

FRIDAY, 8 JUNE 1979

Dear Ty,

The test was so easy I will get at least 75 out of 80 I hope. Well me and Kristi went to the formal and then to the Plankhouse for dinner. The dance was OK. I talked to Dale, shock-of-the-life. I wore my suit and carnation and me and Kristi got six pictures taken so we can give them to friends I know. I hope they give us the negatives so I can get some made if I want to give them to someone else. At the Plankhouse we spent $30.63 on our food for three people and we ate everything in sight. And we went into the bar and went on the disco floor and boogied. I danced with Leslie, a total babe to the max. Lori went home after the dance, what a dud. I thought her parents should have let her go somewhere. Dan did not come. He does not do anything. A real party pooper. Good Night.

Love,
Tony

SATURDAY, 9 JUNE 1979

Dear Ty,

We went to the picnic with Dad and it was so boring it was pathetic. They had a lot of food but it was so shitty I did not eat much. The pool was nice and I went swimming about three or four times. We went in the big LA River (wash). Well tomorrow is the big day, I can't wait to go to Knott's Berry Farm. I called David and told him where to meet me and what time. I don't even know what I will wear tomorrow. I don't have any money and Mom doesn't either so I asked Dad and he said he has some and gave me $10.00 so I am going to take some if I can. I hope so. I have to count my money right now, then to bed. I have to get up at 6 o'clock in the morning to do the papers and get ready. Well Good Night.

Love,
Tony

SUNDAY, 10 JUNE 1979

Missy's Birthday

Dear Ty,

Well we went to Knott's Berry Farm and it was so fun. Monte-zooma's Revenge is so bitchen. It looks like this. First you do the loop and then backwards I thought it would be scary but it was not. David came and his voice has gotten deeper and his cock is pretty big I could not believe it. The tearooms were so dead I saw about three or four cocks but through jeans. I was going to wear shorts but I forgot them in my PE locker and I only have one pair, what a dud. I got to see the annual it is a dud if you want my opinion. People will be so pissed if the cover sucks, the names are spelt wrong. Well it is late, so Good Night.

Love,

Tony

MONDAY, 11 JUNE 1979

Dear Ty,

Well we got our annuals today and I don't think they are bad. Compared to the last two years it is so good. I got a lot of popular people to sign it I was surprised when popular people asked me to sign. I signed as many annuals as I could. I hate signing because you never know what to write but I am getting the hang of it at least. By Wednesday I will be a pro at it. I still don't know what I want for graduation. I either want a Mickey Mouse watch or the book *Marilyn Monroe Confidential*. I have to think of something good to get. I did not get Dan to sign my annual, tomorrow I hope. I want him to sign it so bad. Well Good Night.

Love,

Tony

TUESDAY, 12 JUNE 1979

Dear Ty,

Well I want to ditch tomorrow in the morning. We get our banana split so I want to be there to eat it after we have graduation practice. So I have to go and we will probably take a test in English but I have to miss it if I want to go somewhere and do something. I don't want to go on the last day either, but I think I have to go to practice if I want to be in the ceremony. I got more people to sign today but I still did not get Dan to sign, I will just shit if he does not sign I will go over to his house if I have to to get him to sign. I hope he got one, knowing him he did not. Good Night.

Love ya (ha ha),
Tony

WEDNESDAY, 13 JUNE 1979

Dear Ty,

Well in the morning I went down to the bowling alley and into the tearoom and I sat down and someone was in there and he saw my hard-on and started to jack off and he sucked me and I shot in less than two minutes. This wet dream helped me get off sooner it's about time. Then he stuck his monster cock through the glory hole and he shot right away; his cock barely fit through the hole but it made it. I wonder how come they have not fixed it yet. I want to go down there Saturday when Tyler is there now I can shoot my load down his mouth. We ate the banana split and I sat right across from Victor. It was so much fun at least for me. Then we had practice and it was so hot sitting out in that hot, hot, hot, hot, hot, hot, hot sun. I did not get Dan to sign my book yet, so I have to find him tomorrow or else I will shit. I am going to skate to school tomorrow I hope. Well Good Night.

Love ya always,
Tony

THURSDAY, 14 JUNE 1979

LAST DAY OF SCHOOL

Dear Ty,

I got a tripod for graduation it costs $30.00 I think. Graduation was so fun I had a good time. Then I went to the Round Table to get pizza even though I don't like it. I went there anyway and walked around and talked to people and stuff like that. I did not go in the tearoom once, what a shock-of-the-life. I want to go to the bowling alley but Mom bowls tomorrow so I don't think I will go. I did not know that I could get a work permit at my age. I thought you had to be 16 but you have to be 12 or 13 I think. I am going to try to get one as soon as possible. I did not know I had so many friends but everybody at school likes me almost. If they don't they would be great actors. I am so nice so why should they not like me you know. Good Night.

Love,
Tony

FRIDAY, 15 JUNE 1979

Dear Ty,

Well I did not go to the bowling alley because I got up too late to do anything. I borrowed Pete's 205 mm zoom-telephoto lens and took pictures of birds (close-ups). I hope they turn out. I have to try to write neater starting now. We went to the show and saw *Heaven*

Can Wait and *Players* they were both pretty good I think. I checked out the tearoom and it was boring except I saw some nice cocks, two of them were semi-hard. Tomorrow some of Mom's old friends are coming over, so I can go to the bowling alley and see Tyler again now that it does not take me long to make myself cum. I have to get Dad something for Father's Day. Well Good Night.

Love,
Tony

SATURDAY, 16 JUNE 1979

Dear Ty,

Well I finally got down to the bowling alley and Tyler was there like always and I went into the can and sat on the throne for a while and faked that I came to Tyler and he said, "Let me see," but I pointed it down to the toilet and he left and this other guy came in and would not let me see his cock but I let him see mine like an asshole and it was so dead down in the tearoom. I have to go during the week more. I got Dad something for tomorrow I will wait until tomorrow to tell you what it is OK. I got my porn pictures that I took of myself and they made all the slides. I think I will take good ones now that I have a tripod. Good Night.

Love,
Tony

SUNDAY, 17 JUNE 1979

Dear Ty,

Well I said I will tell you what I got Dad. I got a pipe lighter with his initials on it. It is out of lighter fluid already so I have to get him some lighter fluid. I have decided to shave all the hair off my balls and over my cock for the summer. I am not going to shave because when it starts to grow back it hurts, so I will use Neet and wash it away OK. I am going to call Dan tomorrow and see if he wants to go swimming. I hope he can for a change. We might go camping this month. I hope to go to the beach. "COCK" at the beach I hope. Well Good Night.

Love,

Tony

MONDAY, 18 JUNE 1979

Dear Ty,

Well I did not wait until tomorrow to wash off all my hair I did it last night and it is so weird looking and feeling. I don't have any money so I cannot take pictures of my hairless cock. "Oh Well." I got some clay to make a *Mr. Bill Show* and it will be so hard to do it but I will try to anyway. Why not, I don't know where I will get the money to get it developed but I will get it done, don't worry. I went to Dan's house and he wears a jockstrap all the time and he changed right in front of me with the jockstrap on. Too bad. I called Victor today to get Andrea's number. It was so weird calling him he just acted normal. Well Good Night.

Love,

Tony

TUESDAY, 19 JUNE 1979

Dear Ty,

Well I made my *Mr. Bill Show* now I have to get it developed. I have not paid my bill for my papers and I will be fined if I don't pay it by tomorrow. So I am going to pay it by tomorrow even though I am $17.17 short, Mom will give me credit. Well when I went to get the film I finally got a *Playgirl*. The centerfold is a babe and he has a picture of him hard with his foreskin showing... he is one of the best since Howie Gordon and his ripping hard-on. I wish I could go see Jack tomorrow but I don't have any money so forget that idea. I wish I could fuck or suck some man for money so bad. I would do it so fast I am so goddamn greedy. Good Night.

Love,
Tony

WEDNESDAY, 20 JUNE 1979

Dear Ty,

Well I finally paid my bill and I am not going to give up my route until July 25th so I will have some money when I move. I want to be a male prostitute and make a lot of money. I have a big cock so I ain't got a kid's cock I have a man's cock. I don't know if I would make a lot of money but I will try very hard. I was reading *Circus* magazine and in the classified section they have IDs so I am going to say I am at least 17 going on 18 so I can buy porn books. I hope. I pray. I am going to see if Dan wants to go swimming tomorrow. I hope he can. I am going to try to have a 4th-of-July party. Good Night.

Love,
Tony

THURSDAY, 21 JUNE 1979

Dear Ty,

Well I did not ask Dan if he wanted to go swimming I did not have enough time. I went to this store called Enlightening Experience and these two guys who work there are gay I think. I took an old pair of my pants and cut them off and they show every outline of my cock and balls and when I walked in they looked at my cock and one of them smiled and looked at his friend. I did not say anything like a jackass!! I want to go back tomorrow. We might go to San Diego for three or four days next week. I hope we can go so bad I might get some cock. I might ask Lori to go with me tomorrow and I will be a bisexual, no biggie. I don't know yet. I might, I might not. I will tell you tomorrow. OK. Well Good Night.

P.S. I am going to call Jack tomorrow.

Love,

Tony

FRIDAY, 22 JUNE 1979

Dear Ty,

Well I went to Dan's to see if he wanted to go swimming and he was next door babysitting. That kid is always doing something. I went to Enlightening Experience and they were closed. Then I went to try on some shorts and a little diving suit and I ripped off the bathing suit. I want to get another one soon. Tomorrow we are going to the new house to see it and clean it out because the escrow closed finally so we can move any day now. I am so glad I used to keep my mags in a chest of Mom's and she cleaned it out, today but luckily I have my mags and the ads. THANK GOD for that. Well Good Night.

Love,

Tony

SATURDAY, 23 JUNE 1979

Dear Ty,

Well we went to the new house and my room is so neat I think there are three windows so the room is super light so I hope I can get a lot of plants. I hope so because I love plants so much. Dad said we can get "ON TV" I hope we get it, it will be so bitchen to watch all the movies, especially the R-rated ones. I was going to look around and see the new bowling alley. I am am going to try to put a glory hole in one of the stalls in the tearoom. I asked if Rick next door wanted to go swimming but he did not want to. I will see tomorrow if he wants to and I will see if Dan wants to. Good Night.

Love,
Tony

SUNDAY, 24 JUNE 1979

Dear Ty,

Well I called Jim today and he hung up the phone on me so I am going to blackmail him for almost about $500.00 I hope and if Dad and Mom ever found out I would get in so much trouble. I collected from Mark and I asked him if he thought I was gay and he said it crossed his mind. "Oh Well." I want to go see Jack tomorrow or go to the bowling alley by the new house or go to the Topanga Plaza Mall and try to get a trick. I won't get busted this time, don't worry. I am experienced some this time. I don't know if I should take my skates or not. I probably won't because I can't get a trick on skates. We are going to San Diego Wednesday through Friday. Bitchen huh. I asked Dan and Rick and they could not go dud-ville. Good Night.

Love,
Tony

MONDAY, 25 JUNE 1979

Dear Ty,

Well I went over the hill today and I went to Jack's then to the new bowling alley and there was a vice cop there I think so I left. Then I got on the bus and went to Topanga Plaza and to the May Co. where I got busted and it was dead, and then I went to the tearoom in the Montgomery Ward and I met these two guys that made my cock look like a peanut compared to theirs. Both of them were so ugly it was sickening but I loved both of their cocks dearly while they were in my hands. I got two *Hustlers* and I hid them in the bushes and they are gone and I asked this man who was sort of cute to buy me a *Blueboy* and a *Numbers*. *Numbers* is so bitchen they have bitchen guys in it. I can't wait till we go camping on Wednesday. I want to get it on so bad when we are in San Diego. I am going to take my skates. Good Night.

Love,
Tony

TUESDAY, 26 JUNE 1979

Dear Ty,

Well today I went to Mervyn's and tried on some more shorts but did not get anything. Oh I did get something, a $10.00 wallet made by Prince Gardner and it is a good one for sure and I forgot to tell you that I ripped off the book *Mommy Dearest* from the bookstore in the hardcover. All I had on was a pair of shorts and a shirt, it was so easy, and they are so dumb. Today I went to this men's store by Mervyn's and I tried on super tight bathing suits and I was hard and he saw me and put both hands into his pockets and I just acted like I was doing nothing wrong at all. BS. Well we are going to San Diego tomorrow and I don't know if I will take you with me on the three days. But maybe so. Well Good Night.

Love,

Tony

WEDNESDAY, 27 JUNE 1979

Dear Ty,

Well I decided to bring you along to San Diego. We are at Campland and me, Mom, and Eric have been fighting all day. I knew we would just like last time we were here. I was in the tearoom all day. I saw the biggest cock in my life tonight. The guy was taking a shower and it was soft, and the skin was all wrinkled up, and it was still at least seven or eight inches long. It was the-shock-of-the-life to see one that big. He did not try to hide it either I don't blame him at all. I saw a lot of cocks: some semi-hard ones, some uncut ones (bitchen), and some little and crooked ones, and a lot of others too. We are going to San Diego tomorrow. I want to go to the beach. Good Night.

Love,

Tony

THURSDAY, 28 JUNE 1979

Dear Ty,

Well it is night two at this place. We went to the zoo today and it was okay. I like animals so I had an OK time. Last night we could have gone grunion hunting because it is that time again. Now we have to wait two weeks before we can go again. I saw this huge cock on a kid about my age it was about seven inches long and he was as tall as me just about and CUTE too. There was this guy who has a super bitchen bod to the max, he must lift weights all the time. I saw a lot more cocks than yesterday because I went in the tearoom showers and asked if anybody has seen my wallet that I lost which is BS so I could go in a lot easier than just looking. Well Good Night.

P.S. I brought my skates.

Love,

Tony

FRIDAY, 29 JUNE 1979

Dear Ty,

Well we went to Old Town and it was so boring to the max. And we went to the beach and all the babes hang around down there but they are trying to pick up girls so dead-ville. I was taking a shower and this guy was jacking off in the shower and I kept walking by his shower giving him hints like showing him my hard cock and I guess he was not gay at all. And this guy I saw has a nice bod and had on these super tight pants and he is so GODDAMN CUTE it is sickening. I wish I were that cute but I am no babe but no Frankenstein's monster either. Well Good Night.

Love,

Tony

SATURDAY, 30 JUNE 1979

Dear Ty,

Well I am at home right now and this morning at Campland I was taking a shower and this old man was watching me and he said

I have a nice one and he was sucking me and he took out his cock and it was uncut I almost shit right there and today I sucked my first uncut cock and I loved it. And when we got home, I asked if Lori wanted to go swimming and she could and in the pool I pulled down her bathing suit and she let me, and we went to her house and in the front yard at first we started kissing and then I sucked her boobs and she let me out. I bet she was so shocked when she found out how big I was. Then I put my hand on her pussy and she pushed my hand away. Later, tomorrow, she is going to get up at 5 o'clock. So am I and I will ask her to go tomorrow. My first girl-friend. Well Good Night.

Love,
Tony

SUNDAY, 1 JULY 1979

Dear Ty,

Well Lori came swimming today but I did not have the guts to ask her to go with me. Marco, this guy who lives up the street, asked her to go with him and she said no. I guess she is waiting for me to ask her. I will tomorrow I hope. We did not make out like last night because if her parents ever found out she would be grounded for a year at least and I would never be able to talk to her again, then I would not know what to do. Today we moved some of Dad's stuff to the new house because he is moving in already. I might get a H2O bed (oceanography) because this bed is a piece of shit. Well Good Night.

P.S. I did not get up at 5 o'clock.
Love,
Tony

MONDAY, 2 JULY 1979

Grandma's birthday she would be 79 years old today.

Dear Ty,

We did not even mention that today was Grandma's birthday I don't know why. Well me and Lori did it again and I did not ask her to go yet. Tomorrow for sure. First she came over and then we came and sat on the couch and we started to kiss and we were rolling on the floor and her boobs were out and so was my cock and then I tried to touch her cunt and I unzipped her pants and she said "no please" so I didn't. But when we got up and she had to go home I think she was crying. I think she felt bad about it but she did not act like it at all. But I will ask her to go for sure tomorrow, no matter what. I don't want to move now. Well Good Night.

Love,

Tony

TUESDAY, 3 JULY 1979

Cupid's Birthday

Dear Ty,

Well today was Cupid's birthday and we never did find out if she died or someone kept her. I hope someone has her she was such a sweet little doggie. Today I did not talk to Lori all day so I did not ask her to go yet. I went to Larwin Square today and in front of Thrifty there was this little bird that could not fly and I was going to bring it home with me but this girl took it and I was not going to take it from her. She found it. And there is a nest in a yucca bush in the backyard with five little birds in it. I think it is neat. I am going to send away for a fake ID that says I will be

18 in August (ha ha). I hope I get away with it and get a job. Well Good Night.

Love,
Tony

WEDNESDAY, 4 JULY 1979

Dear Ty,

Well today was the 4th of July and Dad didn't come over and you would have thought that it was any other day of the year. Me, Mom, and Eric got in a super big fight today and I said, "Eric I wish you would just drop dead," and he said "same to you," and I said, "Maybe if I was dead I would not have to listen to your or Mom's Bullshit anymore," and I said, "I might just kill myself to get away from you." I am not crazy I just can't take either one's bullshit anymore. I don't know if I could, though you never know. I am going to write a suicide note right now and let Mom find it accidentally. Then see what she thinks. Well Good Night.

Love,
Tony

THURSDAY, 5 JULY 1979

Dear Ty,

Well I finally asked Lori to go. First she came over and tried to throw me in the pool and Mom was not home and she came in with me. Then we got out and I took off her bra and top then her shorts and then mine. We were out there for about one hour making love. Then she had to go home so she did and then she came back and we came upstairs and took off our clothes and she was going to let me fuck her and I could not get it in and I told her before that I went to bed with someone else and she asked and I said yes and she did not believe me I don't think. I put my finger in her cunt but not the cock. I should have tried harder next time I will for sure get it in. She said she will tell me if she will go or not tomorrow, so I guess I should go to bed so I can fuck tomorrow. Well Good Night.

Love,
Tony

FRIDAY, 6 JULY 1979

Dear Ty,

Well today was a hell of a day. First Lori came over and we are going now and I tried to get it on and she pushed me away, I don't know. Tomorrow. Then Dad called and said, "I want to talk to you," and I think Mom told him that I have been fighting them two or something like that. So tomorrow I find out what happens next. We went to see *Hair* and *The Wiz*. Before we left me and ERIC got in a fight and then I said, "I don't want to go," and Mom said I have to. So I went and I paid my way in then I did not talk to them the whole time we were there. And on the way home I did not say a word the whole way home from over the hill (30 min.) and I just wrote my suicide note and I'm going to try to kill myself by turning on the gas and then just wait but I will call Dad and tell him good-bye and see how long it takes to save me. Well Good Night.

Love,
Tony

SATURDAY, 7 JULY 1979

Dear Ty,

Well I don't know when I will try to kill myself yet, but I told Lori that I turned on the gas last night and showed her the note and she just looked at me. Dad came over and said, "We will talk later." Now I want to know so bad. David might come over Wednesday the 11th and I hope we can go to the disco. I might get some cock, Lori can't go so why not. We did it on the couch but we did not fuck. She wants to take it slow so do I sort of. Dad might get me a waterbed because the mattress I have now is a piece of shit and he said I need a new mattress and I said a waterbed will be just fine. I hope I get one so bad. I will show it off I hope to all my old and new friends. Well Good Night.

Love,

Tony

SUNDAY, 8 JULY 1979

Dear Ty,

Well today we went to the waterslide in Northridge and I made up with Kim, so me, Lori, Kim, Mom, Tony G., and Asshole went. I had a good time there. I wish me and Kim did not make up she is acting like a bitch again. Lori was mad at her when we got home from the waterslide. Me and Lori did not kiss too much today but tomorrow we will for sure. Me, Mom, and Asshole did not have a big fight like all this week. Too bad huh. Tomorrow I am going to jack off until I cum so I can cum with Lori. I have to try hard. I want to go to the bowling alley to get sucked. I am a 100% pure bisexual, no doubt about it, I don't care. Just as long as the gay part stays with me. OK. Well Good Night.

I LOVE LORI.

Love,

Tony

Dear Ty,

Well Lori came over and we fooled around a bit and kissed but we did not fuck. I did not have the time to go to the bowling alley to shoot my load, who cares. I did not take a shower today so I could not jack off till I came. "Oh Well." Wednesday I might go to the Northridge Mall shopping with Lori and her mom and we can leave her mom and her sister and just look around a bit. David called and might be able to stay the nights he is here. I hope Mom says yes. I ain't done nothing wrong so what is the big deal about saying yes or no. Who knows. Well Good Night.

Love,
Tony

Dear Ty,

Well Mom said I can go to the mall with Lori tomorrow. I hope we have fun over there. Mom said David can't spend the night while he is here because Dad thinks we are both gay. He's right but I ain't going to tell him of course. Me and David have been doing things since we were about eight or nine, I guess. Me and Lori did not even kiss at all today for God's sake. This is the first time since we have been going. I wonder why we didn't. I guess we will tomorrow. I want to get a pair of pants at the mall, but no money I think. Well Good Night.

Love,
Tony

WEDNESDAY, 11 JULY 1979

Dear Ty,

Well I went to the mall and I took $20.00 and Mom gave me $4.00 and I came home with the $4.00. I got *We Are Family* by Sister Sledge, *2 Hot* by Peaches and Herb, a 45 and a disco single, *There but for the Grace of God I Go* by Machine, and just a bunch of other junk. David came at about 3 o'clock and tonight we went to the disco and there were no people there we knew but it was OK. I have to get up and dance more. David said his mom would pick us up but she went to LA and we walked halfway home then someone picked us up and brought us home. Me and Lori kissed once all day. "Oh Well." Dad said, "David can't sleep over the whole time he is here." I am going to call and ask why he can't stay. I don't know what we are going to do tomorrow. Well Good Night.

Love,
Tony

THURSDAY, 12 JULY 1979

Dear Ty,

Well David's mom and family came swimming today while Mom was at work and tonight we went skating first and I took my skates and then we went to the bowling alley and played a game of pinball. I went into the can and I was sitting down and looking through the crack at the stand-ups and this guy saw me and went out and came back in and sat down with a hard-on. He started to suck and David came in and he would not do anything so I left and David went in. When he came out, I went in again and he sucked me and I came fast and he let me suck him and he came too. I want to go down there tomorrow all day to suck and get sucked. We might go to the disco tomorrow night I hope so. I will boogie all night. I ripped off a diving bathing suit today from Mervyn's I might get shorts tomorrow. Well Good Night.

Love,
Tony

FRIDAY, 13 JULY 1979

Dear Ty,

Well I got a good pair of shorts from Mervyn's and me and David went to the new waterslide out here it is a pile of junk. We went to the bowling alley and David and Tyler sucked in the tearoom. I really don't care, I did not get sucked but who cares. Me and David went to the disco and there were a lot of people there and a lot that I knew were there. People from Sequoia and Andrea was there and had this strapless dress on and we fast danced about half the night but I was a chicken to ask her to slow dance. "Oh Well." She is going to be in a beauty contest Sunday. I wish I could go, I think I like her. We are going to Dad's tomorrow. I want to go to the beach Sunday. I hope so but you never know. I don't know if I will see David tomorrow. Well Good Night.

Love,
Tony

SATURDAY, 14 JULY 1979

Dear Ty,

Well I saw David a little today and then we went to Dad's. David wants me to go to Magic Mountain on Friday but I can't I know. At Dad's we went to Builders and these two guys came in the store and were gay and the one guy (the cutest one) asked if I could go home with him for a half an hour so I asked Mom if I could go look around and she said yes and the guy's lover was jealous of me (ha ha) so he said, "Meet me in the park at 8 o'clock," and I got down to the park and we went down into the LA River and hid in some bushes and he was so nervous and I sucked him and he sucked me but there were people going by so neither one of us came. When I got home Dad yelled at me I figured that out already. I got a waterbed, how bitchen, and Dad is going to buy it. I can't wait. Well Good Night.

Love,
Tony

SUNDAY, 15 JULY 1979

Dear Ty,

Well today I did not do much. I went to Alpha Beta and I want to cut a glory hole in the tearoom but I don't think I will. I went to Lori's today and we went swimming and then later her dad gave me a ride on his motorcycle. It was OK but I wish he would go a lot faster, but he's a little weird anyway. You never know, he might become my father-in-law someday. Me and Lori did not do too much today but maybe tomorrow. I might go to the bowling alley tomorrow to get some cock in the glory hole. I know I can't go to Magic Mountain with David. "Oh Well." Well Good Night.

Love,
Tony

MONDAY, 16 JULY 1979

Dear Ty,

Well I went to the bowling alley and at first I did not think I would get a trick. Tyler would not go in the tearoom and I sort of wanted to get it on with him sort of. But I never did. Then this cute guy came into the bowling alley and I looked at his cock and he looked at mine. Then he played pinball and I played next to him and he was getting hard. Then he went in the tearoom in the middle stand-up and I went in the sit-down and I was looking through the crack and he got hard then went into the next stall and stuck it through the glory hole and I sucked and he came into my stall and sucked me until I came and I think he fell in love with me right there in the stall. He had the bitchenest bod, hair on the chest and he had a cock about four inches soft but when hard it was about eight or nine inches. I did not see Lori all day, I will see her all day tomorrow. Well Good Night.

Love,
Tony

TUESDAY, 17 JULY 1979

Dear Ty,

Well I went to the bowling alley all day long and did not get a trick the whole time I was there. I did not even see a hard cock except mine. I don't know if I will go tomorrow. I saw Lori tonight and we kissed a little bit and I took her boobs out of her top and was rubbing them while we were necking. Tomorrow me and Lori might go off to some place and get it on. I hope so. I love her so much. Marco borrowed $20.00 and he said he would pay me back tomorrow by 3 o'clock and he gave me all his tapes, which I can sell for about $50.00, and I could use the money—and he said he would give me another $6.00 just for loaning him the money. He is so stupid I can't believe it. Well I will tell you if I get my money or sell the tapes. Well Good Night.

Love,
Tony

WEDNESDAY, 18 JULY 1979

Dear Ty,

Well Marco only gave me $22.40 and I still have three of his tapes. I think I will sell them if I can get down to Tape King. Me and Lori went swimming today and I stuck my middle finger up her cunt and I was going to fuck her but Eric was home so she said no. I wish he was gone so bad but that is the breaks huh. Tomorrow I have to go to the dentist. I know I don't have any cavities because I already looked. "Oh Well." I want to go waterbed hunting so bad I hope we go to a lot of places to look and talk to the guy about buying for once. Well I am a true to life bisexual and that is a fact for sure. Well Good Night.

Love,
Tony

THURSDAY, 19 JULY 1979

Dear Ty,

Well I got the money order for my fake ID. I changed it to say I will be 19 this August 2nd instead of 18 so when I get it I can go buy dirty mags that day and see if I can pass the test. I hope it works. Then I will be 18 and can go to the gay bathhouses. How bitchen would that be huh. We are going waterbed hunting tomorrow over the hill. I hope I find a good one that is cheap. I still want to be a hustler on the streets. I am going to go to Jim's tomorrow morning to make love and then take pictures of me and him then bribe him for money. I don't know yet how much I will get. Well Good Night.

Love,
Tony

FRIDAY, 20 JULY 1979

Dear Ty,

We went waterbed hunting today and I was going to get a double bed but they only make super single or queen size and Dad said he don't think I will like it. "Oh Well." We are going to go to the new house tomorrow. I want to go get the paint and paint. The guy I met at the bowling alley called me today and we have a date for Monday at 10:00 at the bowling alley and now I just remembered that we are going to LA and now I am trying to talk Mom into staying home. I don't want to go anyway. I went to Jim's at about 9:30 a.m. and he was gone already. I will ask him for about $500.00 and that is a lot of money. I will put every penny in the bank and save. I went to Enlightening Experience and the guy said, "Don't you think you will fall out of your pants." I said, "I don't care." I tried to follow him home too but he lost me. "Oh Well." Well Good Night.

Love,
Tony

SATURDAY, 21 JULY 1979

Dear Ty,

Well we went to the new house, Eric and Mom and Me went to a skateboard park and I chickened out. Then I left and went into a liquor store and started to look at the mags and the guy said, "Do you have ID?" and I said no then he said, "Then you can't look." So I put it down and was in the back of the store and this guy was drunk and asleep. So I opened his pants and was going to suck him in public. He was soft but I got him hard and he was a good seven inches. Then these Mexicans said, "Leave him alone," but I acted like I did not understand because they were talking in Spanish. Then he woke up and I ran super fast. I called Jack but did not go over there. I am going to go to the house and paint and order my waterbed. Tonight I went out to Jim's house and this new guy lives there and I looked in his window. He is a total babe. Well Good Night.

Love,
Tony

SUNDAY, 22 JULY 1979

Dear Ty,

Well we went to the new house and I painted my room beige and it looks OK I think. I am going to paint the trim dark brown and my waterbed frame is going to be stained so it will almost match. I was going to go to the bowling alley tomorrow and meet Alan and then cum, but I have to go to LA there is no way out. I hope he calls at 10:00 and we are not gone yet. I might call and just ask for Alan. I don't know. I started to braid my hair it looks so funny. "Oh Well." Mom and Dad said, "I think you should wait to get the waterbed," so I did not order it yet that is the breaks. I am going to ask Jim for $1,000.00 because I will spend at least $500.00 on mags and I need saving money too. I have to go over there Tuesday. Well Good Night.

Love,
Tony

MONDAY, 23 JULY 1979

Dear Ty,

Well we went to LA and I could not go to the bowling alley to meet Alan. I called the bowling alley but they would not page him. "Oh Well." I called the bus place to see how to get to the bathhouse and the guy told me the wrong way so I figured it out by myself. So I have to find a way to talk Mom into letting me go. I will go by myself but she will think different. I hope. The BC bathhouse costs $10.00 for a membership and $3.00 for a locker. I don't think this is a lifetime membership. "Oh Well." My ID did not come I hope it comes tomorrow, I pray it does. Me and Asshole got into a gnarly fist fight today over what to watch on TV. Next time I will beat the shit out of him for real. I hope Alan calls tomorrow so bad. I feel so bad about the whole thing. Well Good Night.

Love,
Tony

TUESDAY, 24 JULY 1979

Dear Ty,

Well my ID did not come. If it doesn't come tomorrow I can't go to BC baths because I won't have an ID. I hope it comes tomorrow. I will tell Mom I want to go to Santa Susana Park to just think about everything that has happened to me and to just think. I know Dad will say yes and I hope Mom does too. But I will go to the bathhouse if they let me go, and on Thursday I don't have a paper route anymore so I don't have to be back by a special time. That is good but I will be home for dinner and before dark I hope if I don't miss any buses. I pray I don't I would just die if I got stranded over there. Mom and Dad would never trust me again as long as I live or longer. I saw Dan today but we did not talk. He was on his bike and going the other way. Well Good Night.

Love,

Tony

WEDNESDAY, 25 JULY 1979

Dear Ty,

Well my ID did not come and if it don't come soon I will write the company a letter. I don't know what I will do tomorrow but who knows. Me and Lori kissed a little bit tonight. I wish we could go somewhere and just be alone. I will ask her if she wants to go to a motel room and be alone for half a day or do something like that. For some reason I don't want to move I don't know why but I want to meet more people and when we move I will meet more gays for sure. I wonder where Don works; maybe he could take me halfway to the baths if he works over the hill maybe in LA I hope. I went to the bowling alley and not one maybe trick…I did not see any cock. Tyler was there but looks like scum and I think his car was at Don's house. Maybe Ty will go to the baths with me. He drives!!! Well Good Night.

Love,

Tony

THURSDAY, 26 JULY 1979

Dear Ty,

Well my ID did not come yet and I think I will die if it don't come and the company is a con. I hope not because I just lost $5.00 down the drain. Me and Lori kissed and she is having her period so we could not fuck. We went to the Sound Factory and we ate lunch at McDonald's and I got a disco single of *Good Times* by Chic, and *One Way or Another* by Blondie, and *Heaven Must Have Sent You* by Bonnie Pointer. I do not have a paper route anymore so after this month I have to do odd jobs or get another paper route. I might go to Topanga Plaza or to the bowling alley I don't know. I might just stay home. I went to Tracy and we just talked about stuff. Well Good Night.

Love,
Tony

WEDNESDAY, 27 JULY 1979

Dear Ty,

I went to Topanga Plaza and this guy picked me up and we went to his house and he had an OK bod and a super nice cock but mine was bigger. My ID came and I went on the bus to the Plaza and I was in the tearoom and he asked how old I was and I showed him my ID. Then he came back after he left, I guess he thought about it and there was another guy. He was 16 and a total babe but he did not like young ones. Then we went to his house and he tried to fuck me and he just pushed hard and it hurt like a son-of-a-bitch then I did not cum. I went home and went to Lori's and her dad took us and she got a pair of tennis-shoe skates and she skated up and down the street. I tried my ID and the guy said,

"That is no kind of ID," and I could not buy the *Hustler*. "Oh Well." I will try again. Well Good Night.

Love,
Tony

SATURDAY, 28 JULY 1979

Dear Ty,

During the day I did not do anything special. Today was Dorian's birthday, Lori's brother, and I gave him my last two goldfish and with all my heart I am so sick of fish. Well almost all of my stuff is packed and tomorrow the Mexican workers that Dad hired are coming to move all the heavy stuff and I wonder if we are going to spend the night and then I will write my first night in our new home. I thought it would never happen. Me, Lori, and Barbie went to the skating rink and it was OK. I took my skates and Lori took hers but she only used hers for a little then rented them. "Oh Well." Well Good Night.

Love,
Tony

SUNDAY, 29 JULY 1979

Dear Ty,

Well the workers came and moved all the big stuff and this is my first night in my new home. This is the only time I have moved except a long time ago and I don't remember that so this is my first time. Tomorrow me, Mom, and Eric have to move all the rest of the stuff because Dad had to go to New York until Thursday. "Oh Well." Oh there is a new song called you guessed it, "Oh Well"

...my song. I wonder when I will get to order my waterbed. They keep saying, "There will be time." BULLSHIT. Tomorrow I hope. I wish I had time to try out my new fake ID and buy some mags. Well that is all for the first night. Oh Me, Mom, Dad, and Eric got into many fights today. Well Good Night.

Love,
Tony

MONDAY, 30 JULY 1979

Dear Ty,

Well this is my second night in our new home and I never want to move again. It is hard work, let me tell you. In the morning Mom and Eric are going to the new house and I am going to stay home and clean the house. Mom and Eric got in fights with me and I took the go-cart, TV, and some of the heaviest boxes off the truck by myself. Dad called and might be home tomorrow night, I hope not. When I asked, "When do I get my waterbed?" Dad had a cow and a half. He said, "Don't worry about that goddamn bed or you will never get it." So I am not going to say a word about the waterbed until he brings it up. I have to find out how to get to BC baths from here I want to go so bad. Well Good Night.

Love,
Tony

TUESDAY, 31 JULY 1979

Dear Ty,

Well guess what...this morning Mom got me up at 10 o'clock to unload the car, then we got the rest of the stuff and Mom went to get her hair done and I went to a liquor store and bought this months *Numbers* and *Honcho* with my fake ID. Then I went to an adult bookstore and got in and they just have a bunch of dirty mags all over the place. I looked at some gay mags and straight ones. Then I looked at movies and you have to keep putting money in them to see the movie. And all these guys were there with hard-ons that are so noticeable and there are so many bulges everywhere. I wish I could get off to go to bed for money don't I wish. Dad got home and all he did was bitch at me right when he got home, so I went to bed. He's such a bastard. Well Good Night.

Love,
Tony

WEDNESDAY, 1 AUGUST 1979

Dear Ty,

Well today I was going to go collecting but I did not get up in time so she left me home and that is tough because I did not want to go anyway. Tomorrow I want to go to Topanga Plaza and get a trick. I hope I meet someone and get some money I am broke to the max. I have champagne taste but a beer pocket and it's the truth to the max. I was going to go somewhere but I did not have any time, but tomorrow for sure. I called RTD so they would send me bus schedules but if I go on the bus I will get them off the bus. "Oh Well." Well that is all for tonight. Good Night.

Love,
Tony

THURSDAY, 2 AUGUST 1979

Dear Ty,

Well today I was going to the bowling alleys and they are two total duds. Then I went to the plaza and I was in Miller's Outpost and this guy who works there is a total babe and I think he had a total hard-on. I want to go back tomorrow. Then I went in the tearoom and I met this guy named Vern and he was uncut and we went and sucked each other off. Then he asked if I wanted to go three-way with his wife so I will call him tomorrow evening and get together with them. He and his wife are rich I think. They know a lot of rich people in Beverly Hills so I might be able to get some rich old bitch to fuck and get her money so I can be a high-paid hustler. How bitchen. He belongs to a ritzy gay club and can get a pass for a day. From now on I have to tell Dad everywhere I go. I want to get some money from Vern. His wife's name is Lana and their phone number is 458-3265. Well Good Night.

Love,
Tony

FRIDAY, 3 AUGUST 1979

Dear Ty,

Well I finally got sick and tired of Mom and Eric's shit so I ran away. Right now I am sitting in the park by Santa Monica Beach. It all started when Eric flicked some Fantastic spray and it got in my eye. So I called Mom and Eric told her I hit him and I didn't then we got in a fight and then I hit him. Then he called Mom and told her and I picked up the phone and said, "I AM LEAVING AND NEVER COMING BACK!!!" Then I got on the bus and went to the baths and it was so weird there. I got sucked by this guy in the orgy room and everybody was grabbing at me. Then this guy gave me some "poppers" and I went on a trip. He said that the five biggest cocks fucked me till they came and I did not remember any of it. I have stayed up all night. This morning I was thumbing and this guy picked me up and we sucked each other off. The first time in a car. It happens more in Santa Monica than anywhere else. Well I only have $7.08. I don't know what I will do. I AM NEVER GOING BACK! Good Night!

Love,

Tony

SATURDAY, 4 AUGUST 1979

Dear Ty,

Well today I got on the Santa Monica bus and ended up at UCLA and there are so many gays down there. First I asked where the tearoom was then I went to a whole bunch of them and I found a glory hole in one but there was practically a line waiting to go in there but me and this cute guy went to an empty tearoom and got each other off. I went to the dorms and they were dead. Then tonight I went down the street and saw some Hare Krishna people. Then I saw Robin "Mork from Ork" Williams and he looked like scum and I was going to get his autograph but I did not have any paper. Then I went back to UCLA Hospital and ripped off a blanket so I would not be cold while I was asleep. At the beach I was sucking this guy and I took his wallet. He had about $10.00 and he caught up with me and I took his money out. Good Night.

Love,

Tony

SUNDAY, 5 AUGUST 1979

Dear Ty,

Well I slept in some bushes and I did not get up until noon. Then I went to the beach and walked around for a bit. Then I went and got my skates and skated. I saw a lot of bulges in jeans and shorts. I saw this guy with green, brown, red, yellow, and a couple of other colors it was so weird. Then I decided to call Vern and ask him for help but he was not home and I did not have the nerve to call home so I came home but I am scared to death to go in the house. So I went back to the park and am going to sleep. Today in one of the tearooms there was this total babe with at least a nine- or ten-inch cock on him and there was this other guy who was following us around who was not too bad and the big guy was sucking my cock down to my balls and I came so fast. Well in the morning I will get my bike and go home. I will leave if they yell at me after I get some clothes. Well Good night.

Love,
Tony

MONDAY, 6 AUGUST 1979

Dear Ty,

Well I came home and Mom goes, "Where were you?" and I said, "At a park." Then Dad came home and my room is all cleaned up and Dad just asked the usual questions, if I thought I was gay, and I said, "I don't know," even though I know I am. He said he is going to keep all my money and we will keep a record of everything I buy. He said I am probably grounded for a very long time and he said that Mom stayed up every night wondering where I was and asked if I would say I was sorry and I said no. Then he said, "Go to your room," and I am not going to leave. So I slept all day long and did not eat dinner. Dad asked how long I have hated Eric and I said "forever," and he did not believe me. "Oh Well." Well Good Night.

Love,

Tony

TUESDAY, 7 AUGUST 1979

Dear Ty,

Well today I went collecting and got $119.00 and my bill is $200.00 and I think I will be short about $20.00. I hope not. I am going to Topanga Plaza to this clothing store called Tops & Trousers. They sell only men's clothes and then I could have a lot of nice clothes and meet a lot of new people that way. Guess what, I want to be a news reporter and do interviews with famous people like Barbara Walters. I want to do interviews with Charles Manson and sell it to *Playboy*. When I was collecting I talked to Marco but no big deal. Then I went to Lori's and Dorian, her brother, said, "Did you runaway?" and her mom said, "Did you have fun on your vacation?" I am going to write a letter to Tom Snyder he is a total pig. Well I hope I get a job so bad. I could use the money. Well Good Night.

Love,

Tony

WEDNESDAY, 8 AUGUST 1979

Dear Ty,

Well I wrote a letter to Tom Snyder but I have to correct it and mail it. I went to Tops & Trousers and got an application and it is all filled out and I will take it back tomorrow. Dad came home from wherever he went and guess what, I get my waterbed next week. I thought I would never get it but Dad said after Mom moves out into the condo. I hope I get the job at Tops & Trousers because I would make minimum wage which is $2.95 an hour so I would work about six hours a day and would make $106.20 a week if I get the job, and $424.80 a month. I would have so much money then I could go on to bigger and better things. I would make $5,097.60 a year then when I am 17 I would have enough money to move out. How bitchen. Well Good Night.

P.S. I pray that I get the job.

Love,

Tony

THURSDAY, 9 AUGUST 1979

Dear Ty,

Well Jeff wrote me a letter and I will write back tomorrow. I called UCLA to see how Lisa is, she just had an operation on her jaw and she is OK. I wrote a letter to Tracy, and one to David. When he goes to his grandma's I will go spend the night at Mom's. If I went over I hope we can go to the disco. I did not take the application back to Tops & Trousers because I called to see the age limit and she said that I am too young because I could not get insurance, but if I could I could work there she said, so I am going to try everything I can to get the job. I will take the application back tomorrow no matter what. Kim said me and Lori could use her waterbed to make it on it will be so fun. Tomorrow I have to go collecting and me and Lori might do it then. Well Good Night.

Love,

Tony

FRIDAY, 10 AUGUST 1979

Dear Ty,

Well today I went to collect and I went visiting and only collected from a few people. I went to get the bus and I missed it so I stuck my thumb out and guess what happened…Vern stopped and picked me up. He asked when I would get it on with them and I said, "I don't know," because I am grounded for who knows how long. Then I got picked up by this man in a van and he gave me a ride over the hill then I skated to Lori's and we got in a fight. Then her mom went to take a nap and her little sister left so we were watching TV and then we started kissing and rolling around the room and stuff like that. Then I called Mom, she came and got me from the corner of LA and Sequoia and Dad was mad because I was gone so long and says someone saw me at the bowling alley and I was not. So he was pissed and now I will be grounded longer I just bet you I will. Well I will tell Vern I am going on vacation so I can't make it. I did not have time to take back my application for the job. Tomorrow I hope. Well Good Night.

Love,
Tony

SATURDAY, 11 AUGUST 1979

Dear Ty,

Well today Mom moved and I had to collect and Mom lives at one end of the Valley and I had to skate to the old house and it took a ½ hour but I told them one and a half hours and went visiting and got to Mom's about 9:30. "Oh Well." I wrote to Lupe, Tracy, David, and Jeff and I have to mail them on Monday because the mailman is a total dick. He does not pick up the mail if he doesn't have anything to bring. I hope I get some brown paint so I can finish painting my room. I have not taken back my application for my job I hope it is still open. Well Mom stayed tonight but not tomorrow. Well Good Night.

Love,

Tony

SUNDAY, 12 AUGUST 1979

Dear Ty,

Well today we went shopping for the first and not the last time. I did not cook dinner we went to Kentucky Fried Chicken. I try not to talk to Eric the Asshole as much as possible. I did not get paint today because Dad slept all day. I have to go get my bike tomorrow from Jack's. I will tell Dad he is a friend of Michelle's and she used to live over here and I know him and asked if I could leave my bike there for a couple of days but he did not know I was running away. I might get to order my bed tomorrow. I hope so, who cares about the paint. Well Good Night.

Love,

Tony

MONDAY, 13 AUGUST 1979

Dear Ty,

Well I finally took back my application to Tops & Trousers and I went to Miller's Outpost and found these super bitchen baggies that are black and I want to get them. I hope I can so I can wear them to the disco. I went into May Co. tearoom and this guy was in there. He was a total babe and had a super nice cock but he was just fooling around so I went after someone else and this other guy followed me to the other tearoom and he had the fattest cock I have ever seen. So we went out to his van and made it and he is opening a flower shop and I will try to get a job there. I got my bike and Jack was not home, thank God. I got my paint and I am done painting so I hope I can order the bed tomorrow. I pray and hope so. Well Good Night.

Love,

Tony

TUESDAY, 14 AUGUST 1979

Dear Ty,

Well all the painting is done now I have to do all the touch-up work. I get the old dresser that is out in the backyard and I can put this big mirror on it so I can look at myself (only kidding). David called and he got my letter that I sent yesterday. He is going to Hawaii on Saturday for ten days and said he will get me some puka shells to wear. I called Lisa and she has a brace in her mouth holding it together or something like that. Me and Lori might do it at Kim's on Saturday. Who knows, we might go to a motel. I wish. I don't know what to say to Lana and Vern. I want to but I don't know what to say. I think there is something wrong with me. I feel so sick and tired all the time. Well Good Night.

Love,

Tony

WEDNESDAY, 15 AUGUST 1979

Dear Ty,

Well I am not grounded anymore. Dad said, "Why don't you get out and see what the world is all about?" so I ripped off some film and then I went skating around and to Reseda Park and took pictures of the squirrels. Then I went to the waterbed place and I went in and the guy looked at me and smiled so I looked at all these big beds and I was laying on the beds. Then he had to see this man to see a new heater. Then I was hard and I sat down and my cock was looking out of my shorts. Then the guy left and he just about came running over to me and asked why I waited so he asked if I wanted to get together and he gave me his phone number, 965-2856. I will call in the morning and meet tomorrow for a suck or fuck. I have to collect tomorrow. Well Good Night.

Love,
Tony

THURSDAY, 16 AUGUST 1979

Dear Ty,

Well I called and his name is Don and I went to his apartment on the bus. First I called and no answer then he answered and told me how to get there. So I left and we were kissing on the couch and he said, "Let's go to the bed," and we sucked and kissed and held each other. Then he tried to fuck me but it would not go in so I fucked him and he came on my chest and I said I came but he asked because I was still hard. "Oh Well." We then took a shower and washed each other and dried each other and I gave him my phone number. He has a lover that lives with him and they might break up. I think I love Don like I love Lori. I collected a little bit and went to Lori's. We did not do anything at all but skate. That's it, I am going over there tomorrow and we will do more I hope. Mom is spending the night tomorrow. I might go to the disco tomorrow night. I hope so. Well Good Night.

Love,
Tony

FRIDAY, 17 AUGUST 1979

Dear Ty,

Well I am at Mom's and I went to the disco with Lori and Kim. I am so shocked that Lori could go because her parents are so strict. We did not even kiss, a total shock. But I had a good time because I love to dance like a wild person. There were a lot of people there. I was on the bus coming to Simi and this guy next to me had a nice bod and I put my hand on his leg at the side then put it on his leg and went for the cock and he said, "Keep your hands to yourself." So that was that. Then I was thumbing and this total dick picked me up and acted so dumb. Then I went to Lisa's and her mouth is wired shut so she could hardly talk. Her dad has the bitchenest darkroom it is color and the neatest lens is 175 degrees. You can hold your hand on your chest and see it looking straight it is so bitchen. Well Good Night.

Love,
Tony

SATURDAY, 18 AUGUST 1979

Dear Ty,

Well I am at home now. Guess what, on Wednesday till Sunday we are going to Reno to the Taglivias'. They are old friends. I want to go to a disco while Mom, Dad, John, and Lucy go to the MGM Grand to a show. I might get a new pair of pants. I hope baggies. We cleaned out the garage today and the man across the alley said, "I see you did such a good job you can do mine next time." He is such a total babe to the max and he has a pretty nice bulge in his tight shorts and on top of that he acted pretty nice and he is a total babe. Don has not called me, I hope he does not give up on me I pray. I hope I can go order my bed tomorrow I doubt it though. I want to get Marilyn Monroe's book to read it on the way to Reno. Well Good Night.

Love,
Tony

SUNDAY, 19 AUGUST 1979

Dear Ty,

Well I did not get to order my bed there was not enough time. We finished cleaning the backyard and the garage. I made a cake and I put them both upside down instead of just on and it split right down the middle and everywhere else. Then we went to Grandma's and Gloria thinks my hair is long enough to roll. I want to get my hair braided so I can wear it like that to Reno and see what people say. Then when we got home we went to Dave's house. It was Shari's birthday, she is 18. Dave and Jackie are going to Reno by plane though. I am reading *Monty*. It's about Monty Clift. He was a sad person. He had so many problems it is sad. In the morning I am getting up at 7:00 to see Farrah Fawcett on a morning talk show. Well Good Night.

Love,
Tony

MONDAY, 20 AUGUST 1979

Dear Ty,

Well today I did a lot of things. First I got up at 7:00 and watched Farrah Fawcett on *Good Morning America*. Then I put mud on my face and it got too hard because I left it on too long and it left my face red and tight, it hurt. Then I wrote Jeff a letter I will send it tomorrow. Then I went to Topanga Plaza to Miller's Outpost to see if they had baggies anymore and they don't have my size so I went to the super expensive store and tried things on while the guy there (who was a babe) kept looking at the bulge in my pants. Then I went to this discount store (Levi's) and found baggies in size 28, 29, 30, and 31, so I could choose which one I wanted and they cost $8.00 less for the same thing. Well that's all. Good Night.

Love,
Tony

TUESDAY, 21 AUGUST 1979

Dear Ty,

Well today we went to Mom's and I finally paid my bill for the Enterprise. It was $200.00 and I spent most of it so I had to take out $50.00 from the bank and I paid for *Bananas* magazine. Then I was going to go to Lori's but we did not have enough time so I could not go. I got my pants finally. I got a pair of baggies, a grey and red shirt to match the black baggies, and a pair of white pants that are just about see-through. If they got wet you could see every inch of me. You can even see the underwear if they were white and they hug my crotch. If I put my cock down my leg I could be a HUS-TLER? We are going to Reno in the morning. I have to get up at about 6:00 or 6:30 in the morning. Well Good Night.

P.S. You are coming.

Love,
Tony

WEDNESDAY, 22 AUGUST 1979

Dear Ty,

Well we are in Reno and staying at this dump of a hotel called The Dunes. On the way up here it was so boring. I read my book *Monty* and I did not even read a chapter then the sun came in the window and I got sick…I don't know what but I went to sleep for about one and a half to two hours. When I woke up we were in Reno. We called the Taglivias' and went over to their house and we are so far away from it. So tomorrow we are going to move to a new hotel, a good one. Vinnie is staying in the hotel tonight and I hope Denise can stay tomorrow and we will sleep together. Me, Eric, and Vinnie threw spitballs all over and made a total mess. I think I am in love with Denise. I would not break up with Lori over it. Well Good Night.

Love,

Tony

THURSDAY, 23 AUGUST 1979

Dear Ty,

Well I sent Lori a postcard of Lake Tahoe and Mom and Dad made us clean up the hotel room and we moved and now me and Eric have to stay in the same bed tonight. We went to Circus Circus and Eric and Vinnie won everything and I did not win anything. Vinnie gave me his elephant so I will say I won it. Then we went to the MGM and went bowling. I bowled a 150, not bad, and we just looked around. Then we went skating and the people down there are so nice. I think it was because I was with Christine and Vinnie; Denise was at her friend's house and then we had to take a cab home. I thought it would be so bitchen but it was no big deal. It cost 95 cents plus ten cents every 1/6 of a mile. Tomorrow we are going to the disco and we might get high if Eric does not go. I hope he does not go. Well Good Night.

Love,

Tony

FRIDAY, 24 AUGUST 1979

Dear Ty,

Well today we went to this place called Boomtown and they are supposed to have a bunch of stuff for kids to do but when we got there it looked just like a casino in Reno. They had a couple of pinball machines and stuff like that. Well we went to the disco called Airways and they dance so much different than at home. They barely move around and scream and jump and have a good time. They thought I was so weird to the max. "Oh Well." Eric went so we could not get high. We spent the night at the Taglivias'. We might go dancing tomorrow. I hope Eric does not go he is such a dud. He barely danced at all, only with Vinnie. Well Good Night.

Love,

Tony

SATURDAY, 25 AUGUST 1979

Dear Ty,

Well we are going to Lake Tahoe but we are going on the way home. We went to this thing called the Flume where you go swimming and it is snow water and so cold. All you do is sit in it and the current takes you to the end. Then you grab on or you will hit the rocks and stuff. We went to Airways tonight and Eric came and I had a cigarette right in front of him. I hope he does not tell. He did not dance once all night and we were there for four hours and I was dancing all over the place. I would ask someone to dance and they would say I dance mighty wild. We have to go to the Taglivias' in the morning to at least say goodbye. Mom and Dad have not said one word about my birthday. I wonder if I am having a surprise party. I doubt it though. Well Good Night.

Love,
Tony

SUNDAY, 26 AUGUST 1979

Dear Ty,

Well we are home and we got to sleep in this morning so we did not go to Lake Tahoe. It only took us about nine hours to get home and I slept most of the way. When we were coming home these two guys were in a truck and I looked at them and smiled and I am pretty sure they were gay. They kept looking in the rearview mirror at me then they went a different way so I will never know. I will get enough tricks in my life. Dad asked what I am going to do for my birthday and I said, "Nothing at all." I think I am going to have a party or something. I called Lori and she went to the show. So I have to call tomorrow. I am going to call Vern and Lana tomorrow. The RTD buses are not running and I can't go anywhere then. Well Good Night.

Love,
Tony

My 15th Birthday
    Dear Ty,
    Well today was my birthday and the most depressing day of my life. First I called Lori and Kim but they had to do stuff and I could not go to Simi and they could not come over here. Then I went to the Balboa Park and it was so dead. Then when I got home Dad yelled at me and asked where I was and said that we were going out for my birthday but now it is too late. Then Mom came over and got me a cake and she lit the candles and Dad took pictures and I kept a sad look on my face. Then Dad gave me a card with $30.00 in it and I was cutting the cake and he said, "Where is what was inside?" I did not say "thank you" right away, and he said, "Forget it," took the money and walked and dropped it on his lap and then he came to talk and I was crying. I want to kill myself and be done with it forever. I pray that I will go to heaven? Please God forgive me? Good Night.
    P.S. Dad said "happy birthday" even if I don't think so.
    Love,
    Tony

Dear Ty,
    Well today I stayed in bed until about 1:00 in the afternoon and then I went to the pet store and got litter and food and tomorrow I am going to wash and wax Dad's car for $7.00 so I can get my hamsters tomorrow. This lady Dad knows came over and Dad said that she is a little weird and he was right she is so dumb. Now I am getting ready to go to bed and they just went out to her car and now I looked out the window and she is sucking his cock and he is licking her pussy out in

the car. Now if Lori came over and we could do it in my room and then he would think I was straight. I called her answering service and they will call at 6:00 a.m. to wake me up tomorrow. Me and Lori better do it sometime tomorrow. Well Good Night.

Love,
Tony

WEDNESDAY, 29 AUGUST 1979

Met Jack one year ago today.

Dear Ty,

Well I got my hamsters finally, a male and a female. The girl is nice and lets you pick her up but the boy is a total bastard. I tried to mate them today but the boy did not know what to do I don't think. I got an application from McDonald's and took it back. I hope they call me, I said I was 16. Today at the pet store the guy who works there had on shorts and no underwear and he is such a total babe. Then at Dale's Supermarket this total babe came in with tight pants and a hairy chest and a total babe. I tried to find some-one to cum with today because I met Jack one year ago but no luck. Me and Lori might go on a picnic on Friday up in the mountains or something so we can fuck in the open air. Well Good Night.

Love,
Tony

THURSDAY, 30 AUGUST 1979

Dear Ty,

Well I got to cum today with a guy I met in Simi on July 23rd. I came out of the pet store and a total babe that works there had on pants but no undies. Then I started to walk my bike and noticed this guy that I had seen before. And then he asked if my name was Tony and it was Alan with a total hard-on and his bitchen bod. Then we went to a school and we could not get in, then we found these super thick bushes and we went in them and laid on all the branches and stuff and both came at the same time. I am getting better. I went to Cal St. Northridge to try to meet someone like at UCLA but no luck. Tomorrow I want to go dancing at the disco I hope I can. I would have to spend the night at Mom's, so what. Well that's all for tonight. I gave Alan my phone number! Good Night.

Love,

Tony

FRIDAY, 31 AUGUST 1979

Dear Ty,

Well I am at Mom's and I went dancing but no one I knew went like Lisa, Andrea, and people like that. "Oh Well." The buses are not running so Dad took me to where Lori's mom works at the spas and one kid spit in my face and I could have just died right there. Then me and Lori went to Sycamore school and fooled around a little bit but there were too many people around. Then Lori's mom took us to the disco and we walked to Kim's to get her and we kissed a little on the way and at Kim's. Then at the disco me and Lori were slow dancing and we were kissing away out on the floor. I am going to go to Dan's and tell him we moved finally and go to Simi Bowl maybe? I don't know yet. I hope the glory hole is still there. It probably is, no doubt. I hope Tyler is there. Well Good Night.

P.S. At the disco I had 13 cigs! No. No.

Love,

Tony

SATURDAY, 1 SEPTEMBER 1979

Asshole's Birthday

Dear Ty,

Well am at home now. I went to Dan's and he went somewhere and I have to call him. Then I went to Kathleen's and she was in the shower. Then to Lori C. and she was still in bed, then to Lori and we just sat around and did nothing at all. Monday on Labor Day Lori and Kim might be able to come over and we will go skating in Balboa Park. I hope they come over! Mom is spending the night and is sleeping on the couch. I don't know why I painted my skates silver! They looked pretty radical I think I want to put flames on them or something. I hope I can find something because they look too flashy. I got another application for McDonald's. I will take it back tomorrow I hope. Well Good Night.

Love,
Tony

SUNDAY, 2 SEPTEMBER 1979

Dear Ty,

Guess what, I got a job! Guess where? At McDonald's. I have to get a work permit from school and take it down there and they will give me a schedule. I am going to try to work Monday, Tuesday, Thursday, Friday, and Saturday during the week 4–8 p.m. and Saturday 9:00 a.m. to 2:00 p.m. or something like that. Tomorrow me and Mom are going to Simi to get Lori and Kim so they can go skating in Balboa Park. Hope Kim does not change her mind like she usually does. I am going to paint my room either blue or green with white trim, and the furniture white with the drawers blue or green. Whichever I paint the room I am going to get a queen single bed. Maybe, I don't know yet. I have to go look some more. Well Good Night.

Love,
Tony

MONDAY, 3 SEPTEMBER 1979

Dear Ty,

Well guess what? Kim changed her mind I am not surprised one bit. Lori was so pissed at her. I think some guy spent the night at her house while her mom and dad were in Las Vegas. My aunt and uncle came over and Marvin is getting so big. Lorainne had high-heel shoes on and they almost fit and I was in my room dancing all around the place. I looked up in the attic to see if I could make a room out of it and it is fucking small for a midget! I am going to get a double bed for sure and no headboard and put shelves up all over the place. Tomorrow I have to call to find out when I can get a work permit and see when I go to register for school. If I work I can't go dancing that much. "Oh Well." Good Night.

Love,
Tony

TUESDAY, 4 SEPTEMBER 1979

Dear Ty,

Well today me and Dad went to register and I took English, Algebra, Social Studies, PE, Driver's Ed, and Photography, and school starts at 8:00 a.m. and gets out at 3:10 p.m. except on Friday I get out at 1:00, how bitchen. I went to this H2O bed place today and on the phone the guy sounded gay and he was…I think the best place is in H2O bed places to find tricks. I have to wait to get my work permit because I don't have my birth certificate. I have to go tell them I did not do anything with the guy because there were too many people around so I just walked out. I was going to call Vern but I lost his phone number and I looked through this and I luckily wrote it down. Thank God. I will call tomorrow I hope. I called Kim and she always goes, "I got to go" and hangs up so I did the same thing and so did Lori. Well Good Night.

Love,

Tony

WEDNESDAY, 5 SEPTEMBER 1979

Dear Ty,

Well today I went waterbed looking and the place was closed and I was down by Topanga Plaza so I went there and I met a guy in the tearoom and I sucked him in the can and guess what, he was a priest. I am sorry God. Then I called Vern and Lana and they said they would pick me up at 5:00 and I was at the mall still. Then I went to the record store and the guy kept looking at me and he was a total babe to the max. Then Vern picked me up at McDonald's and Lana was super pretty then we went to their waterbed and I fucked Lana and it felt so good, better than sucking almost. Then she said she and Vern will do whatever they can to help me and I can come over anytime I want, how bitchen huh. Then Vern took me home and gave me a $20 bill. He said I don't have to take it if I feel bought. I took that money so fast and will take any more that they give me. I might keep it to remember it by. Good Night.

Love,

Tony

THURSDAY, 6 SEPTEMBER 1979

Dear Ty,

Well today I went to the mall and to the record store where that guy works and he was not there and I spent the $20 Vern gave me on records. I got *Cheryl Lynn* by herself and *Step II* by Sylvester and a 12" disco single, *Undercover Lover* by Debbie Jacobs, and a 45, *Bustin' Out* by Rick James. Now there is no more money left. I met this guy when I was walking some of the way home and he was nice but a total scum. I called Dan and he was real nice like always and he works so he can't go dancing tomorrow if I go. I hope I can go and I called Andrea and she might go dancing and Vern gave me four joints and I want to get Andrea stoned. She has never tried it before so now she will. They have some green pot in them so I will try to dry them in the microwave oven. I don't know? Well Good Night.

Love,
Tony

FRIDAY, 7 SEPTEMBER 1979

Dear Ty,

Well I got to go dancing tonight. First I went to the bowling alley and bought a pack of cigs and the tearoom was dead so I went to Kim's and her and her mom were going over the hill so they took me to Jeff's house and Jeff's brother Monty is so prejudiced and he hates Blacks the most. I was going to spend the night at his house but Mom said no. I wonder if Tyler still works at the bowling alley. Me and Jeff walked to the disco and smoked 1 ½ of my 3 ½ joints and I got a gnarly buzz. Michelle got pregnant and she got on Medi-Cal and got an abortion. I feel so sorry for her but that's life she should be more careful. "Oh Well." Guess what, Andrea did not come her mom said no and I cannot go again tomorrow. There was no one there. "Oh Well." Maybe people will go tonight. Who knows. Good Night.

Love,

Tony

SATURDAY, 8 SEPTEMBER 1979

Dear Ty,

Well I am at home at last and I have to get my birth certificate so I can get a work permit. I wonder if I still can get the job. I will fill out another application right there and then and give it to him then. I want a job so bad I want to do it because of the work experience and the money. On Tuesday when school starts I am going to ask people their names like Mark did in 7th grade and say "Hi my name is Tony what is yours?" and stuff like that. I want to meet some cute guys and girls because they will be the popular ones most likely. Maybe if I go to the Ozone, the teenage disco, I will meet people. I hope, but I have to find people to go with first. Well Good Night.

Love,

Tony

SUNDAY, 9 SEPTEMBER 1979

Dear Ty,

Well two more days until school starts I am going to wear my painter pants and a light blue shirt that says, Canon Cameras, on it. I am going to try to get a different PE now I have tennis and volleyball and I want to take swimming. I will see all the cocks in the little bathing suits. And after PE they will shower to get the chlorine off them so <u>cocks</u> galore. Today we went to the show and saw *Hot Stuff* and *The Villain*. *Hot Stuff* was good but *The Villain* was so stupid to the max. Tomorrow I am going to make strawberry jam. I have everything I need so far. All I have to do is cook it. Lori and all of Simi start school tomorrow. I am going to see how long it takes me to get ready for school tomorrow. Well Good Night.

Love,

Tony

MONDAY, 10 SEPTEMBER 1979

Dear Ty,

Well tomorrow morning is the big day. I am going to be so nervous. I am going to try so hard to meet a lot of people and it took me about 25 minutes to get ready that is about right. I am going to wash my hair every morning if I get up on time. Mom and Dad had a big fight on the phone and I know Dad wants to get back together with Mom but I don't know about her. I don't think they will ever get back together? Tonight I was watching *Holocaust* about what Hitler did to the Jews during WWII. It is so sad. I am glad I was born now instead of then. Maybe not? My hamster is going to have babies on Friday the 14th. Thank God Friday is not the 13th?! My room is spotless I hope to keep it that way for a while at least. Well Good Night!

Love,

Tony

TUESDAY, 11 SEPTEMBER 1979

Dear Ty,

Well I went to school for the first day. It was OK. I was too nervous I could hardly say a word to anyone. Tomorrow it will be different. First I have Tennis and Volleyball, second I have Algebra, third my favorite English (ha), fourth my real favorite Photography, fifth this class is so neat Constitutional Law I hope I like it, and lastly sixth Health. I wish I had Driver's Ed first semester instead of second but "Oh Well." I cooked dinner finally. I made spaghetti and Ragu. Some of the guys there are such babes and some of them have super big COCKS. This one guy is a total babe and he is in my PE class. I hope I get to check out his cock. I think my teacher is gay I hope so. Mom came over to ask me if I think I like it over here. She wants me to live with her I know it. Well Good Night.

Love,
Tony

WEDNESDAY, 12 SEPTEMBER 1979

Dear Ty,

Well I went today number two day of school and I am so sick it is sickening. Tomorrow I have to take my camera to school. Walking to school is far to walk every day so I am going to call Vern and Lana and see if they can find someone I can go to bed with and make a few hundred bucks so I can get a moped or something like that instead of bus or walking. It will be so bitchen except I can't bring it home. I will just lock it up somewhere close by like Dale's Supermarket. I will get the best lock I can and then I can ride it to school. That will be so bitchen to the max. I will ask Vern or Lana to take me to get it that will be so fun. I am too sick and tired to call today to see prices. Well Good Night.

Love,
Tony

THURSDAY, 13 SEPTEMBER 1979

Dear Ty,

Well I am still sick but good enough to go car and moped shopping. First I met these two girls and one guy and we went to McDonald's for lunch and I met a lot of people. Then I came home and went to this car place right around the corner and the guy kept looking at my cock and he had a nice one too. I did not find anything really and then I went to this other car place and there were so many babes that work there. This total geek came on to me and then this total babe asked me if I want to go to lunch to get a coke with him and his friend but his car had the back seat out so he gave me 50 cents and said, "Sorry maybe next time." He had the nicest-looking cock. Then I went to this Honda place but I have to go back tomorrow. Then I went to the porn bookstore and this total babe was there and he could have had any girl but he was gay and me and him did it and came at the same time. He said he goes there almost every day so I'll go tomorrow I hope. Well Good Night.

Love,
Tony

FRIDAY, 14 SEPTEMBER 1979

Dear Ty,

Well tonight I did the stupidest thing in my life. First I went to the car place where this total babe works and this other guy comes on to me and was hinting at my cock and gave me his phone number and wants me to call him. Then I went to the porn store and met this guy and we went to his apartment and we both came and he gave me his number and I will call him. Then I came home and ate and then Dad left to a bar so I left out my window to go to the porn bookstore and I forgot my ID but the guy had already seen it so I just walked in and he asked if I had any pot and I didn't so "Oh Well." Then this old man picked me up and he wants to meet me at 12:30 tomorrow on the corner of Sherman Way and White Oak. But Dad was already home so now I am busted and I can't go meet him. He said I can't go anywhere so I can't go meet him. I have an interview at McDonald's at 11:00 a.m. tomorrow morning. I hope I can go still. I hope I don't get grounded for long and I hope Dad does not hit me because I hate hitting. My hamster is supposed to have babies tonight? Well Good Night.

Love,
Tony

SATURDAY, 15 SEPTEMBER 1979

Dear Ty,

Well I went to my interview and I got the job but I have to get a work permit and my birth certificate is not around here so I have to send away for it. He said call when I get a work permit and I have the job. I could not go meet that old man because we went to Santa Monica beach. That is such a fun beach I had so much fun. I jogged about two or so miles at the beach it was not that hard at all. I saw a lot of cocks through pants. I went to the bookstore and Chase, the guy who works there, asked me to go get him a cup of coffee and I did. He is real nice to me. Guess what, I was riding on the wrong side of the street and these cops pulled me over and gave me a ticket and I have to go to the court on October 15th. I don't know why it will take so long. "Oh Well." Tomorrow we are going to Simi and I hope me and Lori can go somewhere? My hamster did not have babies. "Oh Well." Well Good Night.

Love,
Tony

SUNDAY, 16 SEPTEMBER 1979

Dear Ty,

Well we went to Simi and Lori's dad said he was going some-where so I could not come over. I wanted to see her so bad. Her dad is such an asshole to the max. So I went to Jackie's new house and watched them move her stuff. This one guy who helped her was John and he was a total babe to the max and he had on those shorts and no jock or underwear. Then we left and he had some on I think he was onto me I would not doubt it if he figured it out. I did not even call Lori since this afternoon and I know she will be pissed to the max. I should have stayed in Simi anyway. "Oh Well." The bus strike is supposed to be over on Wednesday. We will see I hope so. I have to call Vern and Lana tomorrow. Well Good Night.

Love,
Tony

MONDAY, 17 SEPTEMBER 1979

Dear Ty,

Well I did not call Vern and Lana. I have to remember. Today I went to lunch with Vicky and a bunch of her friends. She is sort of popular and hanging around her I might meet a lot of people. I met this 12th grader who likes her. I think he is sort of popular and he has a super nice cock to the max. We went to lunch at McDonald's and it was OK. I hope I don't get into the habit of going there every day it will get so expensive to the max. Tomorrow I might go to the porn bookstore if I have time and an alibi. Well that's all for now. Good Night.

Love,
Tony

Dear Ty,

Guess what, the bus strike is over for at least 21 days. I am so glad and starting on Monday Dad is going to give me and Eric ten dollars apiece to pay for lunch for the whole week. That will give me two dollars a day and now he only gives me one dollar a day. I could still spend one dollar a day and keep five dollars a week or maybe keep almost all of it. Who knows. I went to the bookstore and the owner or something asked to see my ID and he took it and called the courthouse or something and then he found out it was fake and kicked me out and said, "Never come back you little punk." Then I went to the bookstore on the corner by where Dad used to live and chickened out, then to Jack's store and this total babe works there and I chickened out again. Maybe next time. Well Good Night.

Love,
Tony

WEDNESDAY, 19 SEPTEMBER 1979

Dear Ty,

Well guess what, I went to lunch at McDonald's with this guy who used to like Vicky and his name is Greg and I did not have my money because I spent it and I got an ice cream cone and a $200,000 game piece from McD's and it was an instant win for a Big Mac and I got it. I have never won anything before. Tonight Dad went to a bar and the guy across the alley was walking around in his house and I saw him and I was looking over the gate at him. He has this workroom where he works out and he did not have a shirt on like always. I was praying that he would see me but? I am going to go over there and ask him if he wants to start the *Herald Examiner* so I can see him up close. He is such a <u>total</u> <u>babe</u> <u>to</u> <u>the</u> <u>max</u>. Well Good Night.

P.S. I forgot to call Vern and Lana.

Love,

Tony

THURSDAY, 20 SEPTEMBER 1979

Dear Ty,

Well I forgot to call Vern and Lana so I have to call them tomorrow for sure. I want to get my Honda Express II so bad then I can get around this stupid valley. Today in Swimming I saw some gnarly cocks. I want to be in the other locker room there are more people in there. "Oh Well." Today I went to McDonald's for lunch by myself because no one else had any money. I called Andrea and she was going out to dinner so I have to call back tomorrow. She is never home. I have to try to mate my hamsters again. The county recorder does not have a record of my birth certificate so I have to go to the counselor to get this record. I got a brown pair of cords and two shirts. One says "Disco" and the other says "Jogger's do it early in the morning and sometimes late at night." Well Good Night.

Love,

Tony

FRIDAY, 21 SEPTEMBER 1979

Dear Ty,

Well I finally called Vern and Lana. Vern was not home and Lana said she will try to find someone who will pay for a little lovin'.

I ditched my last class I was too tired to go so I went to McDonald's and ate and then home. The guy right behind us is selling his SUV truck and I acted like I wanted to buy it. He said I could go for a little spin but I said I only had my permit so I can't. Dad is at some bar like every Friday night. I plan on changing my Friday nights' and go to games or dancing. Kim will have her driver's license in January so she can drive everywhere. I want to get a fake driver's license so if I got pulled over I would not get the total bust. Well Good Night.

Love,
Tony

SATURDAY, 22 SEPTEMBER 1979

Dear Ty,

Well I am in Simi and I was going to spend the night at Jeff's but his mom left and Mom had to talk to her before I can spend the night. We walked to Patty's house because she was having a birthday party. So me and Jeff went and it was so dead I could not believe it. Lupe was there and Jill. Jill got a perm and it looks so shitty I can't believe it. She has zits up the butt. I don't see how anybody can even stand her she is ugly, fat, and so fake I can't believe it. Well that's all for tonight. Good Night.

Love,
Tony

SUNDAY, 23 SEPTEMBER 1979

Dear Ty,

Well I am home now and guess what me and Jeff did. First he was not home and I went over there and he was at his girlfriend's and so I went to Gemco (he lives right by it) and looked at stereos and this cute guy who works in the sound room left to the back and came back to the stereos and his cock was running down his leg but he did not make any passes at me. "Oh Well." Then we went to the record department and put some albums we wanted out and we ripped them. I got Rickie Lee Jones, *Off the Wall* by Mike Jackson, and *In through the Out Door* by Led Zeppelin. Now me and Jeff want to take orders and sell them for four dollars apiece and two sets for five dollars. We could make a lot of money. I hope it works. Well Good Night.

Love,
Tony

MONDAY, 24 SEPTEMBER 1979

Dear Ty,

Well today at school I asked some new friends if they wanted some albums for four dollars apiece and I got six orders and one double order so this weekend I have to go to Gemco and get the albums. I took the application to McDonald's on Sherman Way and I start tomorrow at 4:30. I almost got caught because I changed the date of birth but I forgot to change 15 to 16 and almost got caught. I got so paranoid to the max. Well Dad gave me ten dollars this morning and it has to last the whole week. I hope I make it because if I don't I don't eat lunch this week on the days I don't have money. I will make it I hope. Well Good Night.

Love,
Tony

TUESDAY, 25 SEPTEMBER 1979

Dear Ty,

Well guess what, I went to McDonald's like I was supposed to and the lady said that the manager called and Eric said, "He is busy so you can't talk to him" and then hung up and that I don't have the job. I was so pissed that I left and went to McDonald's on Balboa and Vanowen and filled out an application and the lady said I can work if I get a work permit, so tomorrow I will try to get one. Then I went to a porn bookstore and ripped off a gay book called *Stick Shift*. Then I stuck out my thumb and got an instant ride. The guy saw my book and said he was gay too. Then I said, "Do you want to suck my cock?" and we went to the parking lot and he sucked me off two times in a row and then took me home. I might go to Simi on Friday to go dancing. Well Good Night.

Love,

Tony

WEDNESDAY, 26 SEPTEMBER 1979

Dear Ty,

Well I took back the application for a work permit and the lady said it will be ready Friday but I am going to go see if it's ready tomorrow. The sooner I know the better, I hope I get the job I need the money so bad to the max. I called Kim and she got a moped and I am going to call Vern and Lana tomorrow night and see if they found me anybody that wants the cock. I hope people want it because I want to cum when I jack off. I have to daydream when I do it or look at some dirty mags. I don't know what to do. Well that is about all for now. Good Night.

Love,

Tony

THURSDAY, 27 SEPTEMBER 1979

Dear Ty,

Well I got my work permit finally and then I went to McDonald's and the lady said on Tuesday that I could only work on weekends but the work permit said I can work four hours a day so the man said come in on Tuesday and wear black hard shoes and brown pants not cords. So it looks like I really got this job. I hope I have it for a long time so I will have some money. I think I will get $2.90 an hour because that is minimum wage. Well I was going to call Vern and Lana but I did not have time. I might go to Simi and go to the disco I don't know. I hope to God that nothing happens so I don't get the job. The thing for Junior Achievement came and it is Thursday at a junior high on Sherman Way. Well Good Night.

Love,
Tony

FRIDAY, 28 SEPTEMBER 1979

Dear Ty,

Well today was radical. First I did not go to fifth period and Dad was home so I went to Builders then I went to the bathroom and someone came in and turned off the light and it was pitch dark. I turned it on then left. Then I saw this man at a window and he kept looking at me funny and he was a trucker. He left and I ran and caught up to him and asked the time. Dad was still home and we were going to cum here but he had to go and said cum back in one hour so I did and he was not there so I stuck out my thumb and this total babe picked me up and I could tell how big he was but he did not make a pass at me. Then I was cumming home and this man picked me up and was holding himself and we went to this baseball field and he sucked then jacked me off and I saw it cum out of me so that is the first time I have been jacked off. Then the trucker came and we are going to meet next week at 1:30. I kept calling Vern and Lana and it was busy. "Oh Well." Well I am not going to Simi????? Tomorrow I want to go to the Pierce College. Well Good Night.

Love,
Tony

SATURDAY, 29 SEPTEMBER 1979

Dear Ty,

Well today I went to Pierce College and no one was there because of the weekend so I went to Topanga Plaza and there was no one there because most of the stores close at 6:00 and it was 6:30. But I went in this restaurant and asked where the bathrooms were and the guy who told me where was a total fox and the other guy standing there looked down at my cock which was hard and his eyes popped out of his head. Then I came out and was leaving and said "thank you," then the babe came out the door and shook my hand and said, "You will be a fine gentleman." Lori called and we are not broke up yet. I don't want to but maybe it is for the best. Tonight I did not get home till 8:30 and now I am grounded for about two weeks, Dad said. There is a bathhouse close to here and it costs eight dollars for a membership and five dollars for a locker. I might go there on Monday because I filled out this thing that says I am Jewish and will be absent for the holiday and forged Mom's name. I called Vern and Lana and they were not home. "Oh Well." Good Night.

Love,
Tony

SUNDAY, 30 SEPTEMBER 1979

Dear Ty,

Well today I did nothing at all. I guess I am really grounded this time. I bet I get off in a week or so. I got my brown pants for work at McDonald's on Tuesday. I hope I like the job. I can't work the grill and cook and I don't want to anyways. I have to sweep for a little while then I will be cashier and take orders so it is so easy. The cash register has a digital readout and you just punch out what and how many, then the total comes up and you punch in the amount of money and it tells you how much change. I won't even have to think and I have always wanted to do it so it should be fun. I called that guy who works at the car place and we have a date at 11:00 at Shampoo's. I don't know what I am going to do yet. I know I will ditch tomorrow. I want to go to the bathhouse. Well Good Night.

Love,
Tony

MONDAY, 1 OCTOBER 1979

Yom Kippur
Dear Ty,

Well first I went to this porn bookstore at the end of Sherman Way and the guy did not even ask for my ID. I just walked in. Then at this flower shop across the street one of the guys who works there is super cute and has the biggest cock I have ever seen but he did not make any passes at me. "Oh Well." Then the cops pulled me over and I said I lived in Simi and there was no school in Simi and got off. Then I went to Danny's and we ate lunch and he wants me to be his lover and I don't know what I will do. I don't think I am ready for that yet! Then he told me about this bathhouse on Van Nuys and

Victory and he asked if I was going to go. Then he gave me money and said, "Go!" The guy at the door just asked if I was 18 and let me go in and for six dollars you get a room. Then I went looking and this masseur saw me and I fell in love with him. He fucked me and it hurt a little and he came. Then I almost had a heart attack when blood came out of my asshole. It only happens to virgins like me. Then some man sucked me and I came, then I left. I want to go back soon? Mom is here, Dad went to NY until then. Well tomorrow I start work I hope. Well Good Night.

Love,
Tony

TUESDAY, 2 OCTOBER 1979

Dear Ty,

Well guess what? I went to school and wrote a note for being absent and Mom went in and now I am busted even more than before. "Oh Well." From now on, starting tomorrow, I am going to do whatever I am told. I hope so. I have to get up on time, eat and everything, and stop smoking and cussing which will be super hard! Then I will be trusted to do almost anything. Then the bathhouses and no more ditching and I have to try to get super good grades to the max. Well I went to McDonald's and they say I can only work on weekends and this Saturday I work from twelve to eight. Eight hours at $2.90, that is $23.20 a day and $46.40 a week and $185.00 a month just for the weekends. How bitchen that will be!!! I hope Dad lets me work on weekends only? Don called and he still works at the waterbed store. Tomorrow night is Junior Achievement. I hope it is fun. Well Good Night.

Love,
Tony

WEDNESDAY, 3 OCTOBER 1979

Dear Ty,

Well school is so boring and I went to Junior Achivement and it was OK. The people are real nice. We don't have a product yet and we might do T-shirts or terrariums. I hope we do both. Who knows what we will do. I want to run for company president but four other people want to run. And all of them have already been in JA. Well Don from the waterbed place called and I called him at home and his lover answered and now his lover said if it ever happens again he will leave. If he will leave if a friend calls he needs another lover. I don't see how anybody could be so jealous. "Oh Well." Well that's all for now. Good Night.

Love,
Tony

THURSDAY, 4 OCTOBER 1979

Dear Ty,

Well guess what? Dad came home late last night and this morning Dad asked where I went and I said I was at school but just did not go to any classes. Yesterday Eric was suspended from school. I have not even been that busted at school and Dad was pissed more than he was about me forging a note. Tomorrow that truck driver is going to meet me at 1:30 over at Builders. I hope he shows up or he will never see me again and if he does I ain't going to suck him or anything! Danny called (the guy who wants to be my lover) and he said call at 8:00 and I did not. "Oh Well." I don't think I want to be his lover. I don't think I am ready for it yet? Who knows? Well two more days till I work and I don't think Dad will let me work. I hope so. Well Good Night.

Love,
Tony

FRIDAY, 5 OCTOBER 1979

Dear Ty,

Well guess what, first I went to meet the truck driver at Builders and he was there and he said go home and leave the door open so I did. Then I waited and he left like a goddamn FUCKIN ASSHOLE. Then that was over and Dad left and gave me money to go eat dinner and so I called Jack and he came and got me (his lover was not home) and he sucked me for so long then I finally came and he came. Then I went to the porn bookstore and the guy who kicked me out got fired and the other guy knew I was underage and said I could stay anyway. Then the other guy who got fired came in and raised hell so I just left. Then I went to this shoe store and said I need shoes for a costume party and tried on some heels, but they were not big enough so I have to go somewhere else. Tomorrow is the first day? Dad was yelling at me and Eric and I almost said, "We did not ask to move so fuck you," but lucky I didn't. Thank God. Well Good Night.

Love,
Tony

SATURDAY, 6 OCTOBER 1979

Dear Ty,

Well I started work and I HATE IT SO MUCH! First I had to clean tables and then sweep and clean tables then I was so bored to the max. Then I said fuck it and I did hamburgers for a while, then they sent me back out to clean, then I went to the French fry machine and worked there the rest of the night. I walked to and from work and if I work very long I always will. I think I am going to run away again. I hate it here so much to the max. I could go to San Diego with Danny when he moves. I know he loves me dearly so I have to find out when he is going to move and if he wants me to come with. I wonder if I could get my school records sent to wherever I go. I hope so if not I will get a job! I DO NOT WANT TO STAY HERE AT ALL. Well that's all Good Night.

Love,
Tony

SUNDAY, 7 OCTOBER 1979

Dear Ty,

Well first I slept in until 1:00, then I had to mow the grass. Then we went to the Moores' and they wanted to drive the Z (Dan and John) so I got the keys and said, "I don't think he will mind if you drive his car." Then John went into the house and I thought he asked Dad if we could drive the car but he went and answered the phone. Then we left and when we got back Dad was pissed and thinks I said we could take the car. But I didn't I swear to God. Then we got a speech. Eric too because he went along and Dad said write a note why I am mad at him or whatever I am mad at. So I wrote him a four-page note and as soon as I am done I will give it to him. Last night I gave Vern my phone number and Lana will call when they are free. I hope they give me money for a Honda Express II, I pray they do. Well Good Night.

Love,
Tony

MONDAY, 8 OCTOBER 1979

Dear Ty,

Well late last night Dad came in and asked if I wanted to talk and then asked if I wanted to sleep instead and I said "sleep." I know he was mad at the note. "Oh Well." There is this guy in my Photo class and he acts so gay it is not funny. He wears skin-tight jeans and all kinds of chains around his wrists and neck and I think he knows I am onto him. He is real nice and cute but not a total babe. "Oh Well." Tomorrow I am going to ditch and go home with him after 4th period and we might get it on who knows what will happen. I hope we get it on then he will be my first from school. How bitchen! Well Good Night.

Love,
Tony

TUESDAY, 9 OCTOBER 1979

Dear Ty,

Well Greg, the guy in Photo, was absent today, so I hope he is there tomorrow and maybe we can ditch. I hope so. Everybody in Photo knows or thinks he is gay it is so obvious. If I get real close to him he acts as normal as can be. This afternoon Dad went to New York and did not even tell me if he did. I did not hear from him. Now Mom is here and we have to keep everything spic and span. "Oh Well." Well that's all for tonight. Well Good Night.

Love,
Tony

WEDNESDAY, 10 OCTOBER 1979

Dear Ty,

Well tonight I went to Junior Achievement and we finally picked out a product and we are going to make these puppets. They are so funny looking to the max and we got stock to sell. You only have to sell three stock certificates. You have to buy one and Mom bought one and Dad will I hope when he gets home but he probably won't. "Oh Well." Well Greg was absent again I hope he comes tomorrow. I think he is so nice and he could be my first lover. But he is 18 I think he could get busted for getting it on with me. Who knows. Well Good Night.

Love,
Tony

THURSDAY, 11 OCTOBER 1979

Dear Ty,

Well Greg came to school finally. He tried to kill himself. I wonder why? Who knows? Well at least he did not succeed. He is too nice to die so young and has too nice a bod. I hope we can be real good friends and then suck each other to death. Well I ditched 5th and 6th period and went to this girl's house that is in my Photo class and I jogged two miles and this other girl went, P. J., Mary (the girl). Her brother was home and acted like we broke in and he came running out in the nude and he has a super nice cock. "Oh Well." He has an MG midget and he gave Mary, P. J., and me a ride. He goes super fast it was so fun. Well Good Night.

Love,
Tony

FRIDAY, 12 OCTOBER 1979

Dear Ty,

Well today I wore tight pants to show off my cock to Greg but I guess it did not work I hope he figures it out by Monday. Who knows? I pray that he is gay. I ditched again and I have to stop doing that. I went to Reseda Books and to the porn bookstore and you can't get in without a driver's license (Cal) so I can't go there unless it is at night because that guy is super cool and will let me come in. He says no skin off his back, so if I go back it is when he is there. I went to this clothes store to get overalls and the man saw me and rubbed his hand over my cock but I shined him on. He was married so suck that. Well Good Night. We are at Mom's house. Good Night again.

Love,

Tony

SATURDAY, 13 OCTOBER 1979

Dear Ty,

Well today I worked and they taught me how to work the cash register and it was so easy to do. But the girl who was teaching me how to do it is a total bitch to the max. All she did was yell at me the whole time and I was ready to go "I am trying to learn how to do this but if you don't calm down I will just walk out of here bitch." But she is a manager and I would have gotten fired on the spot for that. So I have to be calm. At least I did not have to work lot and lobby. Thank God. Well I worked eight hours today and tomorrow I work six hours. "Oh Well." Well Good Night.

Love,

Tony

SUNDAY, 14 OCTOBER 1979

Dear Ty,

Well I learned how to work drive thru today and the girl (Reana) started yelling at me and I almost hit her this time and I am not a violent person at all! Then they put me on a window and it all went fine. I think it is so neat working down there. But they need to get more organized and the food is never ready on time so the people have to wait forever for their food. I hope Greg comes to school tomorrow. Maybe we will get it on who knows? I hope so. Well that's all for now. Good Night.

Love,
Tony

MONDAY, 15 OCTOBER 1979

Dear Ty,

Well Greg came to school today and guess what? He is gay as me he goes to this gay disco Thursday, Friday, Saturday, Sunday, and Monday. I first asked him if he was going to lunch and he said I could go with him if I wanted to and I did. Then we went to this health food store and at this long table there was a total babe at the other end and he goes, "The blond at the end is a total babe," and that was all it took. I was so stupid not to go for him after we left. Tomorrow if I get the chance I hope so. 'Cause if I do I will attack him so fast and rip off his clothes so fast too. I know he wants it or he would not have taken me to lunch. Who knows. Well Good Night.

Love,
Tony

TUESDAY, 16 OCTOBER 1979

Dear Ty,

Well I did not get the chance to rape Greg today. He went somewhere at lunch so I have to wait till tomorrow I hope. In Photography we were always touching each other. He is 18 and acts like he is 16 or something. Who cares? I do! I hope he does not have a lover or anyone real close. 'Cause that will be me if he don't have anyone. I think he likes me or he would not be friends with me I don't think. Well who knows? I will find out tomorrow if we will screw or something I hope. Well tomorrow I have Junior Achievement and we start our product tomorrow I think. "Oh Well." Good Night.

Love,
Tony

WEDNESDAY, 17 OCTOBER 1979

Dear Ty,

Well me and Greg did not do a thing and he went to lunch and I did not go. There was this band at school today. They were not so good at all but the lead singer and the drummer were total babes to the max. The lead singer had a totally radical cock and didn't try to hide it either. I went to Junior Achievment tonight and we started making our product tonight. I will be able to sell a lot of them. I hope they look sort of like this. They are so cute I think. I want to buy one but might get one free. Who knows. Tomorrow night the Village People will be on *20/20* and I WILL WATCH it or else I will be so pissed. Well Good Night.

Love,
Tony

THURSDAY, 18 OCTOBER 1979

Dear Ty,

Well the Village People were on *20/20* and they (Dave Hodo and Randy Jones) are gayer than I am. The way they talk gives it away right there and then. I will write a letter to David Hodo and see if he writes back I hope he does. I just dream about that body of his so much and especially that cock. I will write it tomorrow I hope. Well nothing much happened at school today. Well Good Night.

Love,

Tony

FRIDAY, 19 OCTOBER 1979

Dear Ty,

Well tonight we are at Mom's and Dad went to some chili thing out in the desert somewhere. I took the bus over here and so did Eric. Then I went to Simi High and saw some old friends. Andrea's hair looks so bad it has been bleached to death! Lupe is having a Halloween party two Saturdays from now and I might go I don't know. I wrote the letter and now I have to rewrite it and mail it. I want to send him a nude picture of me. I don't know though. "Oh Well." Well Good Night.

Love,

Tony

SATURDAY, 20 OCTOBER 1979

Dear Ty,

Well I had to work today and I worked window like always and it was boring as hell. I want to quit as soon as I can get another job and I will. I want to be a bag boy at a supermarket that will be so bitchen. They make four dollars an hour for starts and that is a lot of money. I would dig on that totally. Well we're at home now and I have to work tomorrow so I ain't going anywhere. Well Good Night.

Love,
Tony

SUNDAY, 21 OCTOBER 1979

Dear Ty,

Well I went to work and worked window again but I get paid on the 25th and hope my check is so much but I know it won't be much. Tuesday we have some special test that you have to pass to graduate. Everybody says that they are super easy to the max. Well that's all for now. Good Night.

Love,
Tony

MONDAY, 22 OCTOBER 1979

Dear Ty,

Well nothing much happened at school today. Greg had on skin-tight jeans like always and we are just good friends I don't think we will ever screw or anything. I hope to call Vern and Lana and see when we can get together again. I have to call Danny he probably thinks I have forgotten about him. I don't want to get it on with him that much anyway. I want to get to the bathhouse as soon as I can. I don't have any money so I can't go yet. "Oh Well." Well Good Night.

Love,
Tony

P.S. I came home early today. I am sick.

Love,

Tony

TUESDAY, 23 OCTOBER 1979

Dear Ty,

Well I went to school at 1:00 to take the writing test it was so easy! All you had to do was write two letters and that was it. I know I passed both of them. I hope I did. This girl Lisa and me are getting to be good friends. I hope we become super good friends she is real nice and cute. I am getting to be pretty popular at school but I wish people would call me and I could go out more than just by myself. "Oh Well." I will make a good friend sooner or later? Well Good Night.

Love,

Tony

WEDNESDAY, 24 OCTOBER 1979

Dear Ty,

Today at school was boring like always. After school I went down to this Levi's surplus store and the guy who works there is a total babe and I tried on these super tight pants and the guy kept giving me tight jeans and he said he likes the ones that show off "Peter" best and you can only guess who or what "Peter" is! Then I walked home with him and he is going to buy a Porsche on Friday he hopes. I want to go back and see if he gets his car. I hope he does then he can take me in his car and we can screw I hope. Well Good Night.

Love,

Tony

THURSDAY, 25 OCTOBER 1979

Dear Ty,

Well I had a radical day in Health today. This guy at our table, Craig, is a total babe and wears sort of tight pants. All he did all period was make sick jokes about cocks and cum and he sort of kicked me and we sat leg to leg all period. First he bumped my leg and looked at me and said, "Don't do anything," so we sat leg to leg. Then he showed me the car he had (his dad owns a car company) and he was looking at me funny and smiling real funny maybe he is onto me? I hope so! I should have asked him to give me a ride home. But noooooooooo I'm too stupid! Lupe's party is this Saturday. I thought it was next week, I want to go so bad. Well Good Night.

Love,

Tony

FRIDAY, 26 OCTOBER 1979

Dear Ty,

Well I am going to Lupe's party tomorrow night. I could not find Craig anywhere! I was going to ask him if he wanted to go to the party but I could not find him so I will take the bus and spend the night at Mom's house. I don't even know what I will be. I went to the football game tonight and we won. It was super fun and Dad told me to be home at 10:30 and I got here at 12:00. It was because I went to the dance. It was a total trip. I have to be at work at 7:00 tomorrow morning so I better not be late or I will get busted. I forgot to tell you I got my first paycheck today it was $55.12. I only get 25% that's only $12.79. I don't know how I forgot. Well Good Night.

Love,

Tony

SATURDAY, 27 OCTOBER 1979

Dear Ty,

Well I made it to work on time I don't know how. I got off at 2:00 and then took the bus to Simi and it took almost two hours to get here. I was a punk rocker. I wore this checkered jacket, white pants with red spots on one leg, and braided half of my hair it looked so stupid totally. Lupe and Rodney broke up and Belinda got super drunk and upchucked all night long, That is so funny if she can't handle it why does she drink so much? Victor and Carl got a ride home from Mom. Victor is so nice looking and nice too. Well I called in sick and I can't anymore or I will feel so bad lying like that again. Well Good Night.

Love,
Tony

SUNDAY, 28 OCTOBER 1979

Dear Ty,

Well I'm home now and I think we are moving back to Simi because we looked at some houses and Mom was asking all kinds of questions to the max ("How much? How many square yards?"). I don't want to move again I don't think I could take it anymore and I am getting to be good friends with a lot of people like Lisa, Vicky, Craig, and a bunch of other people and they don't know I rip off or lie or anything bad. So I want to keep it that way and be trusted by all my new friends. I have to get a jacket or else I will just freeze. Well Good Night.

Love,
Tony

MONDAY, 29 OCTOBER 1979

Dear Ty,

Well I went to school today and nothing exciting happened. Me and Craig are getting to be good friends. I don't know if he is gay or wants a close friend to trust and just be real close to. I hope he wants to just be good friends because I ain't ever had a real close guy for a friend and now would be a good time to get a good friend. Well tomorrow we have more tests and they are supposed to be even easier. Well that's all for tonight. Good Night.

Love,
Tony

TUESDAY, 30 OCTOBER 1979

Dear Ty,

Well we took the test today and they ask you how to read a phone bill, how to fill out checks. It was so stupid and some people could hardly do it. I could not even believe it. Me and Craig got done at the same time and he is such a con man. He went in the counseling center and said he had a doctor's appointment and the lady let him use the phone. She is so stupid totally. Well tomorrow is Halloween and I hope I go out so bad! I don't even want to just sit around. "Oh Well." Good Night.

Love,
Tony

WEDNESDAY, 31 OCTOBER 1979

Dear Ty,

Well I went out a little while tonight trick-or-treating with Mary and P. J. I got a lot of candy and I don't even like half of it. I don't like candy that much but what I do like I eat all the time. Craig went to his dad's in Beverly Hills I still don't know if he is gay or wants a close friend. I hope, I pray, good friend. I have people to have sex with. "Oh Well." Well that's all for tonight. Good Night.

Love,

Tony

THURSDAY, 1 NOVEMBER 1979

Dear Ty,

Well today I was going to Panorama City shopping mall but instead I went to Roman Holiday bathhouse. I don't know why but I could not cum. Four different people sucked me and I could not get off. I saw Ben, the guy who works there in the massage room, and he only lives a few blocks away from there and he said, "Call me at home," and gave me his phone number. I will call some other time. Then I was thumbing and this man stopped and sucked me and I sucked him and he had the tastiest cum. "Oh Well." Well that's all for now. Well Good Night.

Love,

Tony

FRIDAY, 2 NOVEMBER 1979

Dear Ty,

Well nothing happened at school today. Oh we saw this radical film of rafting in the Grand Canyon it was so rad. I keep meaning to find out what Craig's phone number is. He likes to go dancing so maybe we will go boogie sometime. Well I was going to go to Mary's mom's boyfriend's and get high and sit in the spa but I was too tired and slept all afternoon. So I just stayed home and watched TV and have to be at work tomorrow morning at 7:00 a.m. and I can't be late. I want to quit so bad! Well Good Night.

Love,
Tony

SATURDAY, 3 NOVEMBER 1979

Dear Ty,

Guess what, I was 45 minutes late to work and I said, "I thought I was supposed to be here at 8:00," and they called here and woke up Dad. Tomorrow I have to be there at 6:00 in the morning and I don't even want to get up that early and I can't be late again or else I might get fired. I am trying to get another job so bad I would rather do anything else than work at that dump anymore. Well that's all for tonight. Good Night.

Love,
Tony

SUNDAY, 4 NOVEMBER 1979

Dear Ty,

Well I was ten minutes late for work again. This man came in and ordered ten cheeseburgers and then changed it to ten Big Macs I was so pissed totally. Me and Dad went to Ted-Mart and I saw this guy Bobby and he is in my Law class and he gets hard-ons all the time in class and he is huge even soft! Finally got a jacket! You can unzip the sleeves and make it a vest it is so nice. Then me and Mom went to JC Penny and I got this super nice sweater. I like it a lot. I am going to wear it tomorrow I hope it looks good on me. Well that's all for tonight. Good Night.

Love,
Tony

MONDAY, 5 NOVEMBER 1979

Dear Ty,

Well I wore the sweater today and Craig wanted me to give it to him so he could wear it tomorrow. I didn't give it to him of course. I went to that Levi's store to look for a shirt to wear with the sweater and the guy who is gay, I could not remember his name and it is Dennis. The other guy called him so that's how I know his name. I found a shirt there and am going to get it tomorrow for sure. I am going to try to dress super nice as I can. It won't happen overnight but in time. I called Craig and he was eating dinner and said he would call me back but he didn't "Oh Well." He probably forgot it anyway. Well Good Night.

Love,
Tony

TUESDAY, 6 NOVEMBER 1979

Dear Ty,

Well I could care less about the election! Well I rearranged my room today and I like it better this way so far. I want to get my waterbed so bad now and I am not going to let Dad forget it either! I talked to Craig today. He gets his braces today and did not go to school and we took the Topics test and it was as easy as all the rest! I called Vicky tonight and we talked for a little bit. "Oh Well." I did not go get my shirt because Dad did not get home in time so I hope I get it tomorrow, if it's still there. Well Good Night.

Love,

Tony

WEDNESDAY, 7 NOVEMBER 1979

Dear Ty,

Well Craig didn't go to school again he said his teeth hurt too much? Well I had to get my thing for the field trip signed and Mr. Hymes, my Algebra I teacher, would not sign so I am going to take truant who gives a damn! I got my shirt finally. It has been raining all fucking day long. I went to JA tonight and we just made more product like always. I think JA is so fucking boring. Well I want to get the song "Rapper's Delight" so bad and no one has it. "Oh Well." Well report cards come out on Tuesday and mine will be so bad? Well that's all. Good Night.

Love,

Tony

THURSDAY, 8 NOVEMBER 1979

Dear Ty,

Well today we went on our field trip to the Supreme Court and it was sort of fun but no big deal. It was different than I thought it would be. Well Craig came to school and his braces don't look that bad at all to me. "Oh Well." Me and Craig were talking on the phone and he was three-way calling on his phone and he called Lisa and all three of us talked. Craig said in Health today that "My best friend is 16 and sits across from me and that's him," so I hope we share all our secrets with each other. I need a friend like him. Well that's all for tonight. Good Night.

Love,
Tony

FRIDAY, 9 NOVEMBER 1979

Dear Ty,

Well school was a bore. But I got kicked out of Algebra I, thank God. I talked to Craig on the phone just about half the night and day and his mom was talking to me and she said I should come over sometime or after school she sounds super cool. She parties with Craig and his sister. Tomorrow I have to be at work at 7:00 a.m. I hope I am not late again. Dad is having his party tomorrow so this house has to be clean and this I got to see. Me and Craig might go dancing on Sunday 'cause there is no school Monday. Well Good Night.

Love,
Tony

SATURDAY, 10 NOVEMBER 1979

Dear Ty,

Well guess what? I quit McDonald's finally. I am so glad I will miss what little money I get but I will find another job I hope. Me and Craig talked on the phone a while and Dad is still having his party right now. I went to Mary's house too and talked a while. She said I shouldn't have even worked there in the first place. She is so right. I can't even believe this house is spotless. I hope it stays that way it looks real nice. Well that's all. Good Night.

Love,
Tony

SUNDAY, 11 NOVEMBER 1979

Dear Ty,

Well Dad had his party and they did not even leave the house a mess I can't believe it. Today my heart started to hurt so bad I don't know if it was my heart for sure but it hurt somewhere around there. Tomorrow there is no school because of Veteran's Day I don't know what I am going to do. I got paint today and started to paint my room. It is this super bitchen color blue. I like it a lot better so far. Well that's all for now. Good Night.

Love,
Tony

MONDAY, 12 NOVEMBER 1979

Dear Ty,

Well I was painting and the phone rang and guess who it was? Alan the <u>total</u> <u>babe</u>. He was at Reseda Park and Eric and Dad weren't home so I met him halfway and he came over and I have been the only guy he has ever had and he said he dreams about me and does not stop thinking about me. I am so in love with him totally. I am not going to go to bed with anyone but him for a while. He was in my room and he was all sweaty and was going to take a shower and Eric came home so he went out my window. I hope he calls me soon. Well that's all. Good Night.

Love,
Tony

TUESDAY, 13 NOVEMBER 1979

Dear Ty,

Well tomorrow report cards come out and I think I am getting Fs in almost all my classes. I hope not Dad will kill me totally. Next Tuesday my Law class is going to this camp where they keep kids who are criminals. I hope all my teachers let me go or I will just be truant no big deal. Well that's all for tonight. Oh Well. Might not go to Las Vegas over Turkey Day. I don't really want to go anyway. Well Good Night.

Love,
Tony

WEDNESDAY, 14 NOVEMBER 1979

Dear Ty,

Well report cards came out and it was so bad I don't even want to tell you what the grades were but I will. In swimming I got a D, in Algebra I I got an F, in English IAB I got another F, in Photography I got another F, and in Con. Law guess an F. And in Health I didn't get an F, I got a D. My grades better come up. Dad said we don't get ten dollars a week anymore and he is going to cut off TV and phones, so if he does that my grades will come up so fast. Craig's was as bad as mine and they have to come up. Well Good Night.

Love,
Tony

FRIDAY, 16 NOVEMBER 1979

Dear Ty,

Well tonight was homecoming and me and Craig went and the tenth-grade float was a skate and we skated in the parade on the track it was so funny and fun. Then Craig borrowed some money from Lisa and she gave him a $5 bill and we spent four dollars and she needed the money because she was going out so Craig gave her $2.50 he was going to use to take a cab home. Then some guy gave us a ride to his house and his sister's boyfriend gave me a ride home. His sister is a total doper to the max, so is her boyfriend. Craig is a total lightweight on pot so am I. That's good anyway. Well Good Night.

Love,
Tony

SATURDAY, 17 NOVEMBER 1979

Dear Ty,

Well today I did nothing at all. I got up at 1:00 and sat around and watched TV a while then talked to Craig for a long time and he did nothing either. I need to get a job again soon so I get another pay-check soon so I don't have to wait until the 25th of the month and it's only going to be about ten or fifteen dollars. Guess what, I forgot to tell you we got "ON TV" but there ain't nothing good on anyway. Well Good Night.

Love,
Tony

MONDAY, 19 NOVEMBER 1979

Dear Ty,

Well school was a bore like always. Tomorrow we are going to Camp Kilpatrick I hope it is OK. I don't want it to be a total dud. I wonder who in our class is going. I hope this guy Bobby goes he gets hard-ons in class and he has a huge cock. I want to become good enough friends with him to check him out every once in a while. Well tomorrow, the field trip. Good Night.

Love,
Tony

TUESDAY, 20 NOVEMBER 1979

Dear Ty,

Well we went to the camp and it is so sad. I would never do anything bad enough to get in there, no way. We got back in time to get to 6th period and me and Craig cut class and this guy Brad gave me and Craig a ride to Ventura and Balboa and we just walked around then went on the bus to Zelsha and I got *Rapper's Delight* by the Sugarhill Gang. Then to his house. I met his sister and mom they are all so weird just like Craigie. Well that's all for tonight. Good Night.

Love,
Tony

FRIDAY, 30 NOVEMBER 1979

Dear Ty,

Well school was OK then when I got home Craig called and asked if I wanted to go to Balboa Park to fly his kite so I went and then I was at Craig's house and called Dad and he was so pissed because of when I was cutting 6th period Thanksgiving week and now I am grounded. That makes me so mad but it's my fault I was truant. I have to stop this shit. Well Good Night.

Love,
Tony

SATURDAY, 1 DECEMBER 1979

Dear Ty,

Well first I did nothing at all, then I went and got five rolls of film and paper so I can make up all my old assignments and get a sort of good grade in there and I finally got a knapsack to carry my books in. Then we went to Moores' house for dinner and all these people came over and surprised Dad and I was going to go somewhere with John and Dan but Dad said I was grounded still so I came home with Eric. Then I watched *Valentino* and some famous ballet dancer starred in it and did a nude scene and he was uncut but I could not tell how big he was because he was soft. "Oh Well." Well Good Night.

Love,
Tony

SUNDAY, 2 DECEMBER 1979

Dear Ty,

Well I finally mailed my letter to Dave Hodo I hope he writes back to me. Me, Craig, and his mother and sister went skating in Balboa Park and it was sort of fun but Dad let me go and I did not think he would and I took a shower before I left and Dad thought I was going to go somewhere else other than the park so Craig came in and finally met Dad so now I hope I can go almost anywhere with him just by asking Dad. Tomorrow I am going swimming and so is Craig I hope. Well that's all. Good Night.

Love,
Tony

MONDAY, 3 DECEMBER 1979

Dear Ty,

Well school went by so fast I could not even believe it. I skated to and from school today and might tomorrow it was not that bad at all. Me, Craig, and gay Greg went to McDonald's for lunch because he asked us and he drove so we went why not. I took a bunch of nude pictures of me tonight I hope they come out. I have to develop the film at school tomorrow. I need to wash my hair in the morning. Me and

Craig did not swim today. I have to tomorrow. Report cards come out next week and mine better be better. Well Good Night.

Love,

Tony

TUESDAY, 4 DECEMBER 1979

Dear Ty,

Well me and Craig got in a fight today, not your little run-of-the-mill fight. We haven't talked on the phone all day and I don't even know why we are fighting. I hope we can be as good of friends as we were a few days ago. Me, Mom, and Eric went and got Dad a nylon shirt for his birthday. He will be __. Can you guess how old he is? Will tell you tomorrow. Well that's all. Good Night.

Love,

Tony

WEDNESDAY, 5 DECEMBER 1979

Dad's Birthday

Dear Ty,

Well Greg called me and I told him I know Dave Hodo of the Village People and he wants to meet him. No way. Me and Craig talked a little today I don't think we will be as super close as we were. I hope so I want us to be friends forever and ever. I put 45 candles on Dad's cake and it almost burned up the cake. I had JA tonight and got three birds and have to build them. Our company is going to go out of business very soon. I hope so I hate it so much. Well Good Night.

Love,

Tony

THURSDAY, 6 DECEMBER 1979

Dear Ty,

Well first Dad didn't get up so I didn't leave until 8:30, then Craig wasn't in school and it was a bore. Then me and Mary went to Jim's house and he asked if we wanted to go in the spa. So we got loaded and this is my first time I ever really have been. It was so weird, I knew what was going on all the time and I was super alert. We were playing a little soccer game and Mary left and Jim got a hard-on so I would see it and we went into the bathroom and got off and Mary almost caught us. I wonder if he is gay, or did it because he was drunk? I will always be over there now. Well it's 1:23 and I called Bob and did not say anything. I am going to prank call them all the time. Well Good Night.

Love,
Tony

FRIDAY, 7 DECEMBER 1979

Dear Ty,

Well Craig didn't go to school again, then I went over there after school. Then Dad came home and he quit his job and now he is mad at us. I know he'll get another job soon. We won't run out of money, no doubt. I went back over to Craig's and we went to Arby's and got free food. Then we went to Karl's Toys and were just fuckin around, then to Big 5 where Alexis works and Craig wants to rip off this jacket. He'll get caught if he tries to. He won't. Dad was mad because I was about 15 minutes late. Well fuck him. Well that's all for now. Good Night.

Love,
Tony

MEMORANDA

Dec. 20, 1978. Went to my first concert and saw Queen at the fourm

~~Jan. 22, 1979.~~ Jan. 20, 1979 - Grandma died

Dec. 25, 1978. Grandma sent her last Christmas card In her life

Jan. 26, 1979. Grandma's funeral.

APPENDIX: DIARY ENTRIES, 1980

A second diary—this one, from 1980—was discovered at the same time as Sean's 1979 diary. Containing only nineteen entries, which take the reader through Sean's sixteenth birthday and first forays into Hollywood, this second diary forms something of an epilogue to the first.

TUESDAY, 15 JANUARY 1980

Dear Alan,

I don't write much anymore I am going to write more because our lives are about to do a number again. First Mom and Dad sat on the couch in the living room, then called me and Eric in there and Mom said, "Me and your father are going to get a divorce," and it almost killed Eric but it did not shock me one bit! Mom was crying her eyes out. Then they said, "You two are old enough to decide where you want to live," so now we have to try to decide if we want to live with Mom or Dad? Mom. And in Van Nuys or Simi. Van Nuys 'cause of Cragie I've never had a friend like him and I don't want to move and ruin it like me and Lori NO WAY! It was a different kind of friendship but not this time. Ni Night.

Love,
Tony

THURSDAY, 24 JANUARY 1980

Dear Alan,

Well today I went on an interview at this modeling agency. It's called International Models Guild Ltd. in Woodland Hills and it costs $500.00 and it is 12 weeks long. It looks like a very good school and I want to go but it starts on this Tuesday and you can pay $150.00 then pay $25.00 a week or pay cash right then and save $50.00 or pay $100.00 and pay $30.00 a week. I want to go 'cause it would be super good experience for me. I wore my Jordache bags and that Oscar of California velour top (it's bright yellow) and I got a pair of Crayons (shoes). I think I looked good enough for this and Mom went with me and she looked good like always. But I don't know if I'll go. I hope so. Well I'm going to sleep now. Ni Night.

Love,

Tony

MONDAY, 18 FEBRUARY 1980

Dear Alan,

Well today was no school so I went job hunting and Dad says I can't get a job and say I'm 16, but there is no other way I can since I'm only 15. But my interview at McDonald's is at 4:00 and this time I'm going to show up. 'Cause Craig seems to be out of my life. But then I was thumbing and this old man picked me up.

WEDNESDAY, 20 FEBRUARY 1980

Dear Alan,

Well I have decided to go away from this place. I want to go tomorrow but I don't know where or when I'm going, so I don't want to leave for good but for a while it will be good for all of us. I'm going to ask Craig if I can come there for a week or so and if I can't go there I'll go to Jim's I hope and if not there I will have to ask Danny if he can do anything. I hope I don't have to go that far.

Tomorrow McDonald's might call me and I hope I get the job so I'll be able to live and eat. If not I'll go to another one, or I will try to sell the speakers. Mom even gave me a bunch of bullshit. But what can I do. Well Ni Night.

Love,
Tony

FRIDAY, 22 FEBRUARY 1980

Dear Alan,

Well today I did a very STUPID thing. I went to Promenade mall to see Dennis at Ann Taylor and then I went to Saks 5th Ave. and tried on a pair of super nice pants and a Calvin Klein shirt and put the shirt in my bag and the pants on and I went out of the store and got change for the bus then like an ass I went upstairs to see Dennis and the store security dude stopped me and that was it. The cops came and got me and called Dad and Dad yelled and screamed at me and I don't think I'll be going anywhere for a while but maybe not. I hope not. Well Ni Night.

Love,
Tony

TUESDAY, 11 MARCH 1980

Mom's Birthday
Dear Alan,
Well Mom worked so we ain't gonna do shit.
Ni Night,
Tony

FRIDAY, 21 MARCH 1980

Dear Alan,

Well guess what, you know I don't write much anymore but I got to now. I didn't go to school today at all. I went to Hollywood and I was on the corner of Santa Monica and Vine and stuck out my thumb and this van pulls over and the guy asked me if I was hustling and I said "maybe" and he said, "Will you suck me for $5.00?" and I said "$10.00" and he said OK and we parked and he had on panties and a bra! Then I wandered around for a while, then stuck out the thumb again and this very good-looking blond stopped and was already hard and he showed it too. Then I sucked him off and he almost made me cum by jacking me off. Then this other guy stopped and he never asked me to do anything but when I was getting out he asked me if I wanted to smoke a joint, so he got me high and dropped me off. Then I walked down to Santa Monica and Highland and this other guy picked me up and said that his roommate and him liked 3-way and they live off of Victory and Sepulveda and he took me to Carl's Jr. and we ate. Then at his house I took off my clothes and he gave me the best head I have ever gotten. Then his roommate got home and his roommate had a HUGE cock and he fucked me and I got sucked at the same time and then all of a sudden I felt like I was cumming and I did and no one even had a hand on my cock and I came all over and so did they all at the same time it was excellent and I am going to call them on Tuesday and I took a shower and was ready to leave and Jim gave me $10.00, so Monday I'm going to open a bank account. I had so much fun today. I'm going to Hollywood more often. Ni Night.

Love,

Tony

MONDAY, 7 APRIL 1980

Dear Alan,

Well I went to school and after school I called Dennis and he already left work so I called Dave and Jim and they had two other guys over there already then Dave came and got me and it was a 5some and the blond guy was sort of cute and me and him just lay there while they did everything it was very good then Dave took me home. That's all for now.

Ni Night,

Tony

MONDAY, 5 MAY 1980

Dear Alan,

Well I'm sorry I have not written in a long long time so. I will tell you what has been going on. First I moved back to Simi and now I live with Mom and I am trying to get my act together for reals this time. But I can't get a job so I have been working the streets for reals just being your typical little hustler boy and I hope I don't get VD or anything like that. It could pay real good 'cause I made $30.00 in a couple of hours and I got fucked and sucked someone and that is more than I would make at any other job. It ain't the best job but what can I say. If I told Dennis he would just die. Well tell you more tomorrow. Ni Night.

Love,

Tony

I love Craig

SUNDAY, 18 MAY 1980

Dear Alan,

Guess what happened yesterday. I was on Santa Monica and Highland trying to make some money, and this man pulls over and I get in then we get to his house and he wants it for free and I say, "But I need the money so I can go to Hawaii for the wedding," and he asked how much it would be and I said "about $200.00" and he asked if I would be his lover if he sent me to Hawaii and of course I said yes and I called at his house and the flight leaves at 6:30 and gets to Honolulu at 8:30. Now I have to go see about how much it costs to get to Maui from Honolulu. And I have to raise that money but I don't think it will be that much. But I have no idea how I'm going to tell Mom and Dad. That is why I have to go to counseling and ask her what I should do but I'm going to tell her it is a lady not a man. Well, Ni Night.

Love,
Tony

TUESDAY, 20 MAY 1980

Dear Alan,

Well I went to my shrink and she said that next week we will tell them when the whole family is there. She said we will tell them it is only a loan from this lady and if they want to meet her I will just die totally. I don't know what I will do at all. I think I might have a party but I don't know. I hope I have a party. Ni Night.

Love,
Tony

SATURDAY, 14 JUNE 1980

Dear Alan,

Well I'm not going to Hawaii because Eddie said it is too risky to give me that money because of my age that is so fucked now I don't know.

SATURDAY, 2 AUGUST 1980

1st year of knowing Vern & Lana

SUNDAY, 3 AUGUST 1980

1 year ago today I ran away from home

WEDNESDAY, 13 AUGUST 1980

Dear Alan,

I know I don't write anymore but I will start now. How can I write a book if I don't know what is happening. Yesterday I worked on Santa Monica and made $30.00 in less than an hour. And today I went to Beverly Hills and I was in Theodore Man and I saw Mike Landon from *Little House on the Prairie* and he kept staring at me and he is so gorgeous and I think he was trying to pick-up on me but I blew it real bad. I thought he was married but he just broke up with his wife I am going to meet him again and this time I will get him. Craig is back and I'm tryin' to get into his pants still. Don't worry, I know that is what he wants. Well Ni Night.
    Love ya,
    Tony

WEDNESDAY, 27 AUGUST 1980

My 16th Birthday
DRIVE!!

FRIDAY, 17 OCTOBER 1980

Dear Alan,

I'm back? I have not been anywhere but I'm so sorry I have not written in so long but I will tell you all the back gossip. First of all I stopped going to school and Mom and Dad know and she kept asking, "What are you going to do?" and I kept saying, "I'll get a job," and I got a job Wed. at Bullock's Sherman Oaks and I worked 6 hrs. yesterday. It was so-so but it is better than going to fucking school. Know what else happened, Granddaddy had a stroke and a week later he died and Mom was a wreck but she is over it more now. Last week Dad went up north and me and Mom stayed at his house and she told me I could not go out and I did anyway and left a note but little did I know Dad would be there when I got there but he was and that next day when I finally got out of bed it was 5:30 in the afternoon and me and Dad had a big fight.

MONDAY, 24 NOVEMBER 1980

Dearest Alan,

If I ever hear from Alan again I'm going to ask him to meet Carol and see if there is any way for us to live together because I don't want to live with Mom anymore and I need to have someone and I think Alan needs me as much as I need him. Tomorrow I go to court for that Broadway card I found I don't know why I am so nervous but I am. The lawyer told Mom there's a 20% chance it will be thrown out of court, or the most I can get is 8 months. Everyone keeps saying, "Don't worry they won't do anything," but I'm a fucking nervous wreck. I will die if I have to go to a camp. A hall won't be half as bad, I don't think. I don't know I am so scared. Know what, I can't cry because I have built up such a strong will not to cry for anyone or anything that now when I want to get the tears I can't. I know if they put me in the hall I will most definitely cry my eyes out but I don't think they take action right then and there because then they make a date for sentencing. Then I would get it but hopefully it will be thrown out of court. I pray it will be.

Love always and forever,
Tony

10·5·81

THE TONY ROBERTSON SAGA
DID TONY EVER COME BACK FROM
THE NILD PARTY IN VENICE?
   OR DID HE GET TAKEN
AWAY BY SOME HIPPIE?
   OR DID TONY FALL INTO A
CANAL AND GET EATEN BY A
BIRTHDAY DOG?
   OR DID HE GET BEATEN
      UP BY A GREASY
         ROCKER?
STAY TUNED NEXT WEDNESDAY
FOR THE EXCITING EPISODE

It is one of the obvious injustices of social life that the standard of culture should demand the same behavior in sexual life from everyone . . . .

— Sigmund Freud

Graphic Design *Barbara Shulman*

UNDERSTANDING HOMOSEXUALITY:
Separating Fact from Fiction

by PROJECT STRAIGHT TALK
on Human Sexuality

This fact sheet was one of several pieces of ephemera tucked into Sean's diary. Based in Los Angeles, Project Straight Talk on Human Sexuality was active circa 1979.

PROJECT STRAIGHT TALK ON HUMAN SEXUALITY

presents

TEN MYTHS AND FACTS ON HOMOSEXUALITY

This Fact Sheet has been prepared by PROJECT STRAIGHT TALK on Human Sexuality, a group of community leaders, many of whom are professionals in the medical, religious and behavioral science fields. We are deeply concerned about the growing prejudice against a substantial segment of our society: Homosexual men and women.

We offer these facts in an effort to combat the myths and misinformation which pervade our society.

We cannot stress strongly enough the need to educate the community so that there will remain a guarantee of Human Rights for each of us—heterosexual and homosexual alike.

1

MYTH

HOMOSEXUALS COMPRISE A SMALL SEGMENT OF OUR POPULATION.

FACT

According to the *Institute for Sex Research (KINSEY)*, approximately 10% of the total population—some 20,000,000 people—is homosexual. This number is equivalent to the entire population of the State of California, the most heavily populated state in this country. They are our *mothers, fathers, brothers, sisters, children, uncles, aunts, friends, neighbors and coworkers.*

2

MYTH

HOMOSEXUALITY IS "UNNATURAL."

FACT

Biological researchers agree that homosexuality is to be found among almost all species, and that it becomes a frequent form of activity among highly developed species. Similarly, anthropologists and historians report that there is practically no human culture from which homosexuality has been absent.

3

MYTH

HOMOSEXUALS ARE EASY TO IDENTIFY BY APPEARANCE, BEHAVIOR AND CHOICE OF OCCUPATION.

FACT

The majority of the homosexual community cannot be identified in this way. Homosexuals are found in all races, all religions, all socioeconomic strata, and in all professions, such as *law, medicine, clergy, education, sports* and *politics*, as well as in *all trades.*

4

MYTH

HOMOSEXUALS ARE MENTALLY ILL.

FACT

As a result of much research, both the *American Psychiatric Association* and the *American Psychological Association* have officially removed homosexuality from the list of mental disorders.

The head of the *National Institute for Mental Health Task Force on Homosexuaity, DR. EVELYN HOOKER,* showed psychiatric tests of homosexuals to a panel of clinicians. These doctors could not distinguish the tests from those of heterosexuals and found no greater incidence of mental illness. *NIMH's* research indicates that homosexual neurotics display the same symptoms as those commonly found among other rejected minority groups.

5

MYTH

HOMOSEXUALITY IS IMMORAL.

FACT

To this day, there is constant dispute among both theologians and lay people of all religions and persuasions concerning the morality of not only *homosexuality,* but of *capital punishment, birth control* and *divorce,etc.* Many religious organizations recognize the significant distinction between church and state and therefore understand that supporting equal rights for homosexuals does not imply a judgment on the morality of homosexuality. Among the religious organizations who are on record in support of equal rights for homosexuals are:

The Lutheran Church of America
The United Church of Christ
National Federation of Priests Councils
Commonweal
The Episcopal Church
The U.S. National Council of Catholic Bishops
The American Jewish Committee (New York chapter)
The Society of Friends (Pacific Yearly Meeting)
The Unitarian Universalist Church.

6

MYTH

HOMOSEXUALS RECRUIT CHILDREN

FACT

Neither homosexuals nor hetereosexuals can ''recruit'' children. Sexuality is an innate part of a person's personality, and not a chosen orientation. Experts, such as *DR. JOHN MONEY* of *Johns Hopkins University,* agree that a child's sexual orientation is determined by age three or four. Major studies such as those done by the *Institute for Sex Research (KINSEY)* show that it is generally impossible to change sexual orientation once it has been determined.

The President of the *American Psychiatric Association, DR. JOHN P. SPIEGEL,* commented, ''Some have feared that homosexual teachers might affect the sexual orientation of their students. There is NO evidence to support this thesis.'' (Emphasis added.) School officials in cities with anti-discrimination policies confirm this in their reports.

7

MYTH

HOMOSEXUAL TEACHERS WILL BE HARMFUL ROLE MODELS FOR OUR CHILDREN.

FACT

As stated above, most sex researchers today agree that sexual orientation is determined before children enter public school (at three or four years of age); therefore, homosexual teachers are not able to influence a child's sexual behavior. To paraphrase one adult homosexual male: "In all 12 years of my public schooling, I had only heterosexual role models as teachers and they did not influence me one iota in being heterosexual."

If societies had always discriminated against homosexuals as teachers, we would have been deprived of such outstanding role models as *ARTISTOTLE, PLATO* and SOCRATES.

8

MYTH

HOMOSEXUALS ARE CHILD MOLESTERS.

FACT

By far, most acts of child molestation are committed by *heterosexual males*. Child molestation is NOT related to sexual orientation according to all studies done by governmental agencies. The Director of the *Children's Division of the American Humane Association, DR. VINCENT DeFRANCIA* reports, "There are 10 girls molested to every boy; 97% of the offenders are male."

9

MYTH

HOMOSEXUALITY WILL LEAD TO A DECADENT SOCIETY.

FACT

The acceptance or non-acceptance of homosexuality has no bearing on the rise or decline of any culture and no reputable historian since the 18th century has taken this theory seriously. Our notions of homosexuality as socially destructive derive from ancient societies that put a premium on increasing the population.

We view as socially destructive
...lowering the economic value of homosexuals to the community as a whole by depriving them of equal working opportunities
...burdening the taxpayers with welfare recipients who are denied jobs on the basis of sexual orientation
...paying for prison upkeep for those charged with victimless crimes.

As may be seen, anti-homosexuality, not homosexuality, appears to be more socially destructive.

10

MYTH

CIVIL RIGHTS FOR HOMOSEXUALS WOULD GIVE APPROVAL TO HOMOSEXUALITY.

FACT

Such legislation seeks only to protect the rights of a substantial portion of the population. It would not endorse, encourage or approve homosexuality. All it would do is guarantee homosexual Americans the right to work in a job for which they are qualified...to live in housing they are able to afford...and to live in freedom as law-abiding citizens—rights which are guaranteed to *everyone else.*

For further information contact:

PROJECT STRAIGHT TALK on Human Sexuality
2210 Wilshire Boulevard, Suite 326
Santa Monica, California 90403
(213) 661-3292

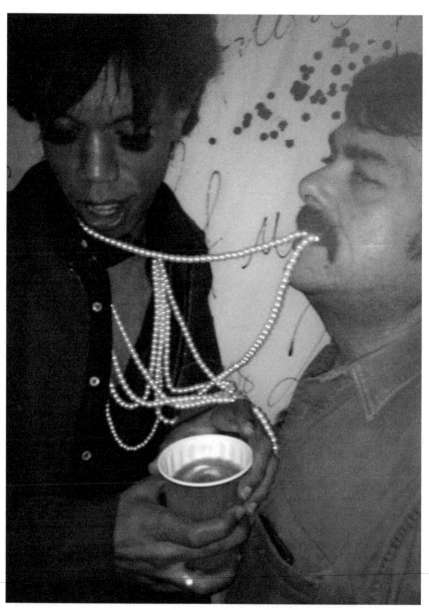

Sean DeLear and Cesar Padilla at Cowboy Gallery, 2014. Photograph by Brett Eugene Ralph.

Hitching a Ride to Heaven

Like everyone else in the Southern California basin that didn't fit in where they were from, Sean DeLear had to get out! It was sometime in the mid-1980s that I first saw Sean roaming the dark old bars and clubs of Hollywood, East Hollywood, and Downtown Los Angeles that at that time housed the outlaw scenes of punk culture. My earliest vision of Sean that really sticks out is from sometime around 1987–88. I had seen him before—at punk shows and the edgier gay bars—but this vision was special. We were at a club called Candilejas, on East Sunset by the Children's Hospital. It was 1:45 in the morning, the club was closing, and people were spilling out onto the streets. Sean was wearing a wig—or was it his real hair? I'm not certain—and there were champagne flutes in it rigged with wire to float in the air. He was sitting on a bike saying his farewells, and then went riding off into the night, heading east on Sunset. He was so graceful as he rode away. In my mind, the bike has a low seat and tall sissy bar, but maybe that's my fantasy.

Sean De defied gender and had a blast doing it. Fearless and androgynous in appearance, Sean often worked both sides of the fence, toying with conventional masculinity while accentuating his feminine traits. Roddy Bottum once told me a story about Sean that in many ways says it all. Roddy and his sister Stephanie met Sean De very early in the LA punk scene. Stephanie had a young daughter, and when the daughter once met Sean De at a function she innocently asked him, "Do you want to go outside, He-She? What's your name? He-She?" Sean enjoyed blurring the lines. He loved to fuck it up: he in fact relished in his signature, casually androgynous identity.

I don't remember Sean ever introducing himself as Tony. To me, he has always been Sean De. By the late '80s, Anthony was something from the past; Sean DeLear was the future. I asked him on one occasion his real name, but by then Anthony/Tony was far behind him. He had evolved. Artist Richard Pursel, another friend of Sean's since the mid-'80s, recently told me he remembered the day Sean had his name legally changed on his driver's license. Tony vanished.

When Sean De passed away in Vienna after a short-lived battle with cancer, I volunteered to go help his fiancée, Markus Zizenbacher. I flew to Vienna and dealt with the coroner, morgue, crematorium, the paperwork, receiving a crash course on how to deal with a dead body overseas. As Markus and I started packing up Sean De's belongings, I came across the text you hold in your hands. I read a few pages and was blown away. This is the complete diary, as it was written. A gorgeous, naive, innocent yet horny nubile fourteen-to-fifteen-year-old's fearless journey of self-identification, hustling, cheap thrills, danger, Donna Summer, and so much more. A diary not written with any literary aspirations in mind, but rather a teen's uncensored document of pre-AIDS gay punk Los Angeles, with all the fun vernacular of a bitchen awesome and gnarly kid from the San Fernando Valley desperately hoping to get "over the hill" into LA, with side trips to the local porn shops, glory holes, and swap meets.

For kids growing up in the San Fernando Valley, getting "over the hill" meant salvation. Escape from the vanilla suburbs at all costs. Hollywood was a magnet that drew the outsider kids in. Come to Hollywood, change your name, and be who you really want to be. Everybody is a star; you can be one too or die trying. Sex and danger were everywhere on the streets of Los Angeles circa 1979. AIDS was just around the corner. We were post Charles

Manson and his angels, and coming of age with the Hillside Strangler. Los Angeles was filthy and tawdry back then. The streets of the city were dangerous for kids.

As I read this journal, I realized Sean and I shared a lot. I'm a post-hippie sun-kissed smiling pot-smoking cock-sucking gay Chicano punk, raised just south of Downtown Los Angeles, past the stinking industrial cesspool of Vernon. I'm just a couple of years behind Sean, but I too sucked dick and fucked at my regional bowling alley, frequented glory holes and adult book stores, but on the Latino side of town.

I loved it. I loved walking the commercial streets of my neighborhood boiling with teen lust. I got my cock sucked in the front and back rows of the grindhouse theaters of Huntington Park, South Gate, Maywood, Bell Gardens, California, etc. I knew the parks, dark corners, train tracks, and best bushes back then. This book screams of cum-quenched insatiable nights of life before the Meese

Commission, the US government's 1986 raid on pornography. How lust and danger went hand in hand. Hitchhiking was a legit form of travel. Getting in cars with older men sounded fucking fun. Getting sucked off as well made the ride even better. Still does.

I remember this Los Angeles that Sean writes about and that the Moral Majority was afraid of. When getting a ride to Santa Monica Boulevard and West Hollywood meant a night of illicit jizz-drenched action. Scantily clad youth spilled onto the boulevards—as in Santa Monica, Sunset, and Hollywood. Thumbs out, Daisy Dukes on, hitching a ride to Heaven or maybe even around the world or maybe just to the nearest parking lot. Saying, "Hey mister, have you got a dime? Hey mister, do you want to spend some time?"

Fake IDs were easy then. Catch a ride to Hollywood Boulevard and a dozen or more shops churned them out at a pittance for the freedom they promised. Just south of Sunset Boulevard, on the west side of Vine Street, was the old Greyhound station. Every day, pretty much every hour, a bus would pull up from some *Last Picture Show*–type town with young, erupting, hot-blooded teens, male and female, with one-way tickets to paradise, running away from the repressed life they knew. It was a one-way bus to stardom.

It is hard to separate, as a Los Angeleno, where the glamour of Hollywood starlets and Hollywood meet the dirty streets, where our obsession converges with reality. In many ways to us, they coexist perfectly. I often think about Sean De's posture. He stood so regally. Always upright and never slouching. Sean carried himself like a star. He *was* a star—a star out on a stroll in casual drag, so to speak. A little of the shoulder, those big-ass eyelashes, and a swinging cock.

I am quite positive Sean De's graduation from life's beauty academy and cotillion came with his on-site education at the hands of Susan Tyrrell: for a time, Sean shared a flat with the Academy Award–nominated actress. "SuSu," as she was called, was on her way out, having suffered bilateral below-the-knee amputations. Bless her heart.

I, too, love Old Hollywood decaying glamour. We all love a good fall and I am also from the wrong side of the tracks. I too knew I was not the son my mom wanted. When I first found this diary, I understood right away Sean's need to get away and stay away. I also understood the need for this diary to exist in book form. As I delved into the diary further, I began thinking I was reading the most honest book I had ever read. This diary has no pretense: it's just an amazing Southern California kid's story, plain and simple. A kid who grew up to break down many walls, go seamlessly from scene to scene, party to party, city to city, country to country, to be known eventually throughout the Western hemisphere in the underground art world. These pages represent and speak clearly of this person's fearless beginnings.

I carried the diary with me on the plane back to the States from Vienna. As I sat down for the flight, I fell asleep and dreamt that

Sean DeLear was my flight attendant. Dressed in a midnight-blue, Jackie O–inspired 1960s flight-attendant suit with a matching midnight-blue Halston pillbox hat, Sean De was rocking his signature fake eyelashes, accentuating those huge Diana Ross eyes of his. When I woke up in tears at the beauty of this vision, it was clear that Sean De's spirit was with me. I had his back and now, in the afterlife, he had mine. I was carrying him home in this book.

Upon my return to New York City, I called a gathering of some punk gays in our creative circle. It happened that a number of Sean's friends were in town. Roddy Bottum, Ron Athey, Mike Hoffman, Michael Bullock, and a couple of others all met up at my apartment and read aloud from this diary, passing it around so each could read a few passages. As we read these pages out loud, it became clear that this book was something very special. Days later, Michael Bullock approached me about publishing the book.

I was having a conversation the other day with Ron Athey. Ron had recently spoken to our dear mutual friend and our elder, the artist Philip Littell. Their conversation consisted of how in our day and age—meaning the youth of Philip, Sean, Ron, and myself—we, as gay, either went the faggot route or the artist route. Those were our options. Were we going to be retail queens, florists, interior decorators, or any of the other few options an out gay man had in those days? Or were we going to use this gift to create something radical, something both personal and culture changing?

Sean De managed to bridge both of those worlds effortlessly. I decided to call Philip to break this down a little. He responded, "The faggot imprisons the artist these days. With Sean, there was an absence of affect. He wasn't asking for acceptance. He just was. Did he ever work? Part of his artwork is not doing any work, but just being. His artwork didn't have an objective, so like his life it didn't do any work. His work very purely exists for itself. It is work devoid of responsibility. He carried this notion in his life. He was so

nonchalant about living his truth. It wasn't a put on. There's a lot of terrific gay art with a lot of purpose to it; there are things that crusade for different things. But it's rare when someone just says, 'I'm me—that's all you need to know.' As a performer, a lot of his style was to look as if he barely cared. Today, a lot of energy goes into self-identifying. The work carries with it defiance and outrage and self-dramatization. But with Sean, or with Warhol, you see them having a *delightful* time, whatever is coming down—and you can join."

Sean blurred all the lines and became the Art. His life became a walking, evolving performance piece. He carried himself like a movie star, pretty much at all times. Yet he wasn't in any way precious or fancy, nor did he fancy himself fancy. He wasn't a diva, yet he was a diva. He lived for fun and a good time. First and foremost, Sean was Punk Rock for Life—and royalty, at that. It's an aesthetic you're born with. He walked the walk. You can't shake it.

Sean DeLear (1965–2017) was an influential member of the "Silver Lake scene" of Los Angeles's 1980s and 1990s before moving to Europe. In Vienna, he became part of the art collective Gelitin and devised a solo cabaret show, *Sean DeLear on the Rocks*. DeLear was a cultural boundary breaker whose work transcended sexuality, race, age, genres, and scenes. As Lina Lecaro wrote in the *LA Weekly*, "Sean DeLear epitomized everything that ever made me want to write about Los Angeles nightlife … He was Los Angeles royalty."

Michael Bullock is a Brooklyn-based writer, editor, and political organizer. He's the author of *Roman Catholic Jacuzzi* (2012) and the editor of *Peter Berlin: Artist, Icon, Photosexual* (2019). In 2020 he founded the political crowdfunding platform WeeklySenator.org, of which he is the director. Bullock also holds the position of associate publisher for *PIN–UP* magazine and contributing editor for *Apartamento*.

Cesar Padilla was born and raised in South Central Los Angeles. He is a self taught Chicano writer, filmmaker, curator and musician and owner of the vintage fashion archive CHERRY. He has directed music videos for legendary Mexican metal band Brujeria. He is the author of *Ripped: T-shirts from the Underground* (2010). Cesar's band, The Ritchie White Orchestra, is currently working on their 4th record.

Brontez Purnell is a writer, musician, dancer, and director based out of Oakland, California. He is the author of several books, including *Since I Laid My Burden Down* (2017) and *Jonny Would You Love Me If My Dick Were Bigger* (2015). He is the front man for the punk band The Younger Lovers and founder of the Brontez Purnell Dance Company. In 2022 Purnell received the Lambda Literary Award for Gay Fiction for his latest novel *100 Boy Friends*.